WILL
FERRELL

WILL FERRELL

STAYING CLASSY – THE BIOGRAPHY

RYAN HUTTON

JOHN BLAKE

Published by John Blake Publishing Ltd,
3 Bramber Court, 2 Bramber Road,
London W14 9PB, England

www.johnblakepublishing.co.uk

www.facebook.com/Johnblakepub facebook

twitter.com/johnblakepub twitter

First published in paperback in 2014

ISBN: 978-1-78219-764-5

British Library Cataloguing-in-Publication Data:
a catalogue record for this book is available from the British Library.

Design by www.envydesign.co.uk

Printed in Great Britain by CPI Group (UK) Ltd

1 3 5 7 9 10 8 6 4 2

Papers used by John Blake Publishing are natural, recyclable products made
from wood grown in sustainable forests. The manufacturing processes
conform to the environmental regulations of the country of origin.

Every attempt has been made to contact the relevant copyright-holders,
but some were unobtainable. We would be grateful if the
appropriate people could contact us.

CONTENTS

CHAPTER ONE

WHEN THERE'S A WILL THERE'S A WAY

The accepted wisdom is that comedians are not what they appear to be. Beneath that smile and wit that leaves audiences gasping for breath as they cry tears of laughter is a twisted knot of neuroses and low self-esteem.

The accepted wisdom is that comedians have come to rely on humour as their protector – their shield that has manifested itself from a childhood filled with taunts from classmates and a troubled domestic life.

That is the accepted wisdom.

Will Ferrell, who was born John William Ferrell on 16 July 1967 in Irvine, California, is a comedian. In fact, he's arguably the most famous funnyman on the planet. And he's the exception to the accepted wisdom.

On paper, he seems like every normal comedian. He wants to make people laugh. He has a desperation to do so, and has left no stone unturned finding ways to do just that. He has pretended to be like a cat, he has stripped off several times, exposing his flabby flesh to the millions, he has pulled faces, endured physical pain and spent hours upon hours obsessively making sure his comic creations were just right for public consumption. But the personal demons that plague other comedians never quite materialised. He wants to make people laugh. That's it. As he has said before in an interview to About.com, 'A lot of people have gotten into comedy because of certain influences in their lives or events that were painful, and I really have racked my brain to figure it out. I pretty much have had a normal childhood. Maybe it was too normal.'

He was born to two caring parents – Betty Kay, a former schoolteacher, who taught at Old Mill School and Santa Ana College, and Roy Lee Ferrell, Jr, a musician with The Righteous Brothers. The group, with vocals from Bill Medley and Bobby Hatfield, had several hits including 'Unchained Melody' and 'You've Lost That Lovin' Feeling'. Forming in 1962, they split up after six hugely successful years together, but the two singers failed to find the same success as solo artists. They eventually reunited six years later.

Will said about his parents to AintItCoolNews.com: 'It's funny because my Mom and Dad actually have a very good sense of humour. Also, I wasn't your typical class clown or anything like that growing up, but if anyone dares me to do anything, I'll do it in two seconds … if I feel like it.' He added: 'I kind of had a relatively normal upbringing, so there are no real traumas to look back on. No bitter, tortured comedian here. Maybe it's just that growing up in suburbia, sitting back for no other reason than wanting to analyse things comedically. Maybe it just comes from that general boredom you sometimes get.'

Betty and Roy both came from Roanoke Rapids, North Carolina – a town in Halifax County which is located near the Roanoke River. They met in second grade, and fell in love – and decided to move to California in 1964. Will said to *Premier Magazine*: 'Dad's a musician. He's keyboard, saxophone, and vocals. And I kind of watched the entertainment industry though his eyes and his experiences – the ups and downs of life in nightclubs. He came out here initially, then he brought my mom, and they lived down in San Juan Capistrano at a motel. Dad played music and Mom was a cocktail waitress.'

Despite moving to the Golden State, Betty made sure her hometown formed an integral part of her children's childhood. Will and his younger brother Patrick regularly headed to Roanoke Rapids during summer visits to see his Uncle Bill in Lumberton, an aunt in Cary, and another aunt in Raleigh.

While Will is more adjusted than other comedians, he was still prone to using humour to deflect moments of weakness. When he was eight years old, his parents divorced – a traumatic situation for any child. However, Ferrell, no doubt bruising inside, chose to show a different facet in front of people, looking at the bright side and telling everyone that he was delighted, because he would now have two Christmases.

The strain from his father's showbiz job – which saw him touring for months on end – has often been cited as the reason for the marriage breakdown. And the long patches of not seeing his father would have understandably caused Will to look at the world of showbiz with some concern. He said to Front Row, 'In looking back, it's what I always wanted to do. But I was suppressing that urge because it was unthinkable. It's too hard to get into comedy, acting, movies or whatever –too unpredictable. My father's a musician, and I had seen how he could work at a nightclub for a year and then come home one day and be like, "Well, they said the job is over." "What happened?" "Nothing, they just said they are going in a new direction." And I thought, "That's no way to live." So I was dead set, like the rational part of my brain, even as a little kid I was saying, "I'm going to get a real job." I didn't know what that was, but I had the image of walking around with a briefcase. That was having a real job.'

As traumatic as a parental split can be for the children, it seems both parents successfully ensured that Will and his brother were loved, and that the impact it had on them was as minimal as it could be. Will's sunny disposition certainly helped the parents cope with the upheaval. But his anger did come out every once in a while. A neighbour had to repair a window after young Will reacted with fury when a kid took the seat off his Big

Wheel, with Will grabbing the seat back and throwing it at the kid, only for it to whizz past him and smash through the neighbour's window. He also shoplifted once, stealing a spare pack of Monopoly money from a local drugstore after he grew frustrated that there weren't enough 500-dollar notes in his board game. It was the first time he stole, and the last. (*Rolling Stone*, 6.3.2012)

Irvine is a city in California, and one that has developed a reputation as one of the best places to live in America. In fact, because of its good schools and jobs it was ranked as the fourth best place to live in the United States. Irvine was a safe place to live – the kind of suburban utopia that were seen in the early films of Spielberg – a place where kids could roam outdoors and goof off without getting in too much trouble. The city's mission statement is to 'create and maintain a community where people can live, work, and play in an environment that is safe, vibrant, and aesthetically pleasing'. Will said (*Orange County Register*, 23.7.2008) about his hometown: 'Growing up in suburbia, in safe, master-planned Irvine, there was no drama so we had to create it in our heads. My main form of entertainment was cracking my friends up and exploring new ways of being funny. I didn't have to have the survival mode instinct like other comics, who grew up in tough neighbourhoods. I had the opposite. For me, I grew up in Mayberry, and the humour broke the boredom. And there was a lot to make fun of.' He also added: 'The Irvine PD [Police Department] loved giving bike tickets because they didn't have a lot to do. That always amused me.'

He attended school at Turtle Rock Elementary, before going on to Rancho San Joaquin Middle School. In first grade he learned a trick, something that would yield an increase in popularity instantly. He would open a door and have it hit the bottom of his foot, but by snapping his head back at the right point, it would look like the door had smashed him in the face. Perfecting the move saw him make the other kids laugh, garner new friends and even serve as an icebreaker with girls. Humour was a way for Will to test himself – to see how far he could go. Once he turned up at high school in his pyjamas just to see if he actually had the nerve to go through with it. Ignoring the occasional sneers and negative attitudes from classmates, he honed in on the ones that he made laugh, reasoning that they were the ones in the majority and that he made more friends with his humour than not. In an interview with *Orange County Register*, he said: 'I was never a class clown or anything like that, but I do remember being in the first grade and my teacher, Mr Chad, told the class one day that we were going to do some exercises. He meant math exercises, but I stood up and started doing jumping jacks. To this day, I don't know what possessed me to do that, but all my friends cracked up. That was invigorating. Of course, later it was all about making girls laugh.' He also explained to NewsOK.com: 'I was a good student, and yet, I describe myself as a conscientious class clown. I would have fun up to a certain point, and then if the teacher gave me a dirty look, I'd be like, "I gotcha," and I'd back off.'

Comedy was something that he grew up with – admitting to the website Den of Geek: 'I think I got a general love of comedy from my parents in a way. And then I loved the first, original cast of *Saturday Night Live*. I just thought that was a collection of five or six comedic actors that were so good that it's amazing to think they were on the same cast. ... My dad turned me on to Peter Sellers as a kid. I loved the fact that he was a unique combination of being extremely subtle and over-the-top all at the same time, and that's a hard thing to do. I admire that. The other influence is Steve Martin. When he came on the scene, he was doing silly comedy that didn't follow a linear path – if you were to write down what he was going to do, it wouldn't make sense. I think that's inspired my generation, and it's happened a lot of times when writing a script, and the studio ... [In *Anchorman*] DreamWorks wanted to take out the Steve Carell character, Brick Tamland. "He doesn't make sense! Every time he speaks, he doesn't make sense! Lose that character." But that was the point. That's why he's in there.'

He added: 'I used to love watching *The Tonight Show* with Johnny Carson. Anytime there was a comedian, I'd try and watch it. Obviously *Saturday Night Live* – Dan Aykroyd was my favourite. I like that he was so versatile and yet he could support and could be really funny. He could kind of do anything. Another person I'm a huge admirer of is Tom Hanks just because he's the Jimmy Stewart of American cinema right now. Everyone forgets that he started out on *Bosom Buddies*. And he's a good dramatic and comedic actor as well. It'd be fun to do that kind of transition. Kind of what Jim Carrey's trying to do. That'd be great if you can make that jump and people allow you to. Phil Hartman too in the same respect as Aykroyd.'

During senior year, Ferrell would perform several comedy routines over the school's intercom system with his friend. 'I'd be up late at night writing them. I never ad-libbed,' he remarked. Writing his material, and receiving the blessing from his principal, Will began to hone his talent – adding to it by performing routines in the school's talent shows, winning the Best Personality honour in a vote by classmates. In an interview with *Front Row* magazine, he remarked: 'I just loved comedy, I really did. I just started making my friends laugh; I always had a funny group of friends. We'd just do stupid stuff. We were the kids who instead of going to the high school party and getting drunk and drinking all the beer, we were going into the person's freezer and defrosting his parents' frozen food and handing it out to people. Just doing weird, bizarre, almost Andy Kaufmanish stuff to entertain ourselves. And I think that's what fostered my "style", if you will.'

It's no surprise that he favoured the wild antics of Andy Kaufman, the late trail-blazing comic who was famous for antagonising his audience and deliberately incurring the wrath of diners in restaurants by walking up to a couple and demand she leave the man to go with him because 'he was famous' – something she would do – leaving fellow diners open-mouthed in shock and having to comfort the broken-hearted man, not realising that it was all a well-organised joke – something the diners would never know. Will told *Index* magazine: 'I love Andy Kaufman. When I first heard about him reading *The Great Gatsby* from cover to cover on stage, I was like, "God, that would be so much fun to do!" I love that kind of thing. It's really fun to make people laugh, but there's a small part of me – about 20 per cent – that doesn't care if the audience thinks something is stupid. I get almost as much pleasure out of that kind of reaction. In a twisted way, I enjoy it when I'm doing a sketch and it's just bombing. It makes me want to slow down and take my time, like, "If you hate it this much, I'm going to make it last even longer."'

When asked by *Rolling Stone* magazine whether he has ever had adolescent angst or self-loathing, he said: 'No way, not even close.' In the same magazine, he recalled an embarrassing encounter with his mother after she feared that he had slept with a girl that she didn't approve of. He hadn't, but she still insisted that if he had, he had best put a 'condom on that pecker of yours'. Despite his reputation for acting the fool, Will was not bullied at school – mainly because of his size and sporting prowess. At University High School in Irvine, Will Ferrell was a field-goal kicker for the school football team. He would spend hours and hours kicking a football through goal posts, requiring him to be in, as he puts it, a 'Zen-like meditative state'.

He said to the A.V. Club: 'I played a lot of soccer, and then they needed a field-goal kicker, and then I found myself on the varsity team as a sophomore. It's a high-pressure, high-stakes position, unless you play for the high school I went to. We were 1-8-1 my senior year, so not a lot of field goals kicked. I think it was four for six. It was just six attempts the whole year. Adam McKay [future director of many of his films] always jokes, because he feels I'm very good under pressure, or I would never break when we were doing *Saturday Night Live* – he was like, "it's 'cause he's a field-goal kicker".' Sport would play a big part in his life in his formative years – thanks mainly to his mother who believed he was the perfect size for playing soccer. A strapping lad, he excelled at soccer and he was also the captain of the basketball team while at high school.

In 1986, he graduated from University High School – alongside other notable alumni that included Dita Von Teese. His pals, so used to Will's zany antics reverberating around the town in Irvine, expected their funny friend to make a name for himself far outside the reach of a small town. Comedy wasn't quite ready for him yet, however. Instead he enrolled at the University of Southern California, studying Sports Broadcasting. He said: 'By the time I was ready for college I didn't know what to do. I think I secretly wanted a show-business career, but I was suppressing it. I liked watching sports so I went in that direction at USC.' (*Orange County Register*, 23.7.2008) He couldn't keep his joking side clear, however. Examples included streaking round campus, and dressing in a janitor's outfit and walking into his friends' classes. He remarked to HamptonRoads.com: 'I'm not a dance-on-the-tables kind of guy. I mean, in college I was known to streak a few times, but I don't need to do that stuff. But if someone dares me to do it, I'll do it in two seconds. It's not that big a deal.'

Asked what was his craziest USC campus memory, Will replied to AboutMovies.com: 'Let's see, I had a fair amount. I had a work-study job in the Humanities AV [Audio-Visual] Department. I was in charge of checking out tapes and overhead projectors and things like that. No one really kept track of where I was. I could leave my job at any time and what I would do on occasion is I would find out what classroom certain friends were in and then dress up as a janitor and show up in the middle of class. There was one specific class that I would do it to. I don't know if they have Thematic Option there any more, but it was kind of a high-level English class and the teacher actually encouraged me. He would see me on campus and say, "Come by in two weeks and just screw around." I would stand outside the door with a power drill and just pretend like I was working on stuff, so I'd do stuff like that.'

While he was at USC, he also partook in that very American university tradition – joining up with the Delta Tau Delta Fraternity, a fraternity that had been founded in 1858 in West Virginia. Notable celebrity members include Matthew McConaughey and Drew Carey. According to their website, the 'Delta Tau Delta wants bold leaders interested in leaving a legacy on campus. With the support of a brotherhood over 150 years in the making, you will have the chance to redefine "fraternity" on your campus. What will you come back to in 20 years? What type of stamp will you leave on campus? With Delta Tau Delta, the choice is yours. Fraternities are values-based organisations that offer young men many challenges and opportunities a traditional college education does not. Through leadership opportunities within a fraternity, a young man can gain leadership skills that will be valuable after graduation. A member of a fraternity has an immediate support group that will become lifelong friends. Joining a fraternity is more than just something you do in college. It is a commitment for a lifetime.'

A fraternity is an organisation that groups men together and prompts companionship and brotherhood. Once you join a fraternity you bond with them for life. While it has its serious side, there are also many playful sides to being a frat-boy – evidenced by the stereotype of fraternity antics that include hard partying and initiation pranks played on potential new members. Will joined the fraternity as an excuse, according to a 2003 interview, to 'try out bits on my friends'. He held the title of Song Chairman during his time as a member at the fraternity. He also jokingly proposed that the fraternity 'goes gay' so it would save money on throwing parties to attract women. Will said in an interview with *The New York Times*: 'Half the guys thought I was really funny. The other half were like, "What's his problem?"'

He told *Empire*: 'Some friends and I would go to Vegas and commandeer a blackjack table and pretend we were travelling businessmen who didn't know each other. There were people sitting in between us who were real civilians and we'd just do these bits. During *SNL* [*Saturday Night Live*], we'd go out to bars and do stuff. One night I almost got beat up. I was doing "magic" and I would not-so-subtly take the staff's tips off the tables. Then Adam [McKay] world come over and ask if I was bothering the customers. Then he'd try to take the tip!' The divisiveness of his talents would be something that would be repeated many times over the years.

At that moment Will had no idea what the future held for him. Sports seemed to be a natural fit – he had the education and physicality for it, but he still had that nagging feeling that there was something else, that there was something more he was destined for. He loved making people laugh – be it at him or with him. He enjoyed the thrill of creating humour, particularly in places that weren't a natural fit for comedy. He had caused havoc at university, fraternity and school, using humour to command attention. He remarked to *Orange County Register*: 'I wrote an essay in the second grade about what I was going to do when I grew up, and I said I was going to be a professional soccer player. In the offseason, I wrote that I was going to be a comedian. So there was a little seed there.' But comedy never felt like a natural career path. It was one thing to cause comedy chaos with impromptu routines, it was another to suddenly try to forge an actual working life from it.

But it was his parents who, despite their relationship troubles through the hardships of showbiz life, would take him down the unsteady path of a being a career comic.

CHAPTER TWO

STAYING
GROUNDED

Despite his natural talent for making people laugh, it was sport that seemed to be the logical career step for Will. He graduated with a bachelor's degree in Sports Information in 1990, and he even earned an internship in the sports department at a local television station. However, that internship proved to be a negative experience – and it would fuel his decision not to pursue a career in broadcasting.

Instead of a sports broadcasting career, he worked on a number of jobs, including stints as a hotel valet, with a second-day disaster after he drove a van under a low-lying beam, knocking the baggage rack off the top of the van. Another job saw him working as a teller at Wells Fargo, but that didn't go so well after coming up $350 and $280 short in the first two days – as a result of incompetence, not theft. A year of this saw him disillusioned, and his mother encouraged him to pursue something he loved. As a Christmas present he was given nine weeks of acting classes by his mother. It was a gift that would change his life.

He told NewsOK: 'I absolutely loved it. And kind of at the same time on my list of things to do in life was to try to do one night of stand-up comedy. ... I'd always been able to make my friends laugh and then I was starting to make strangers laugh. And then I thought, "Oh, maybe I can do this."' He would perform small comedy sets in Irvine, but his surreal brand of comedy wasn't quite to the taste of the fairly conservative-minded town. He explained to *Premiere*: 'There's an improv down in Irvine, two minutes from my house. I would go and I would sit in the back of the room on their open mike nights and gauge. "I think I'm as funny as that person." But I didn't have the guts enough to get up there. But I did a stand-up comedy workshop in an Irvine Valley College extension course catalogue. I thought, "Oh my God, this is perfect." It will force me to have to get up and perform. The six weeks ended in a performance at the old Golden Bear down in Huntington Beach, which I think is torn down. That was the kindest audience ever, people in the class and family and friends, I thought: "Oh my gosh this is fantastic. I'm a natural." So my first time in front of a real audience was a place called The Barn, in Tustin. It wasn't promising at all. The TV blaring in the corner, guys playing pool while you're standing up there with a microphone. I got so nervous that all of the moisture left my mouth, so I couldn't keep my upper lip from sticking to my teeth. And I kept going "gaack". I sped through my material, then "Thanks for coming. I'm Will Ferrell" – just flop sweat, the worst. I drove home and went, "Mom, how do you think it went?" She went "I think you did really good. You have a nice presence, but you have a bad tic." And I said, "Mom, that's because all the moisture left my mouth!"'

In 1991, he decided to move to LA. As for many others, it was initially a struggle. He went to a scene study, where he was met with ruthless feedback – being told that, not to be mean, but he wasn't really any good. He recalled to Backstage: 'I remember going to one of those casting workshops, where you pay 50 bucks and go off and work on scenes. I came back and they evaluated me, and the guy was like, "Conservatively speaking, you need three more years of work, probably working at our workshops." I was like, "Uh-huh, OK." Not to say that he was wrong and I was really good, but it just felt creepy and weird. Also, in the limited amount of commercial auditions I used to do, I swear every time I went in, the person in front of me would come out laughing with the casting director. They'd be hugging each other: "Bye, Bob! Great to see you! Say hi to the wife!" Then they'd be like: "Next! Phil Ferrell!" "Uh, it's Will, actually." "Whatever."'

However, Will believed that you have to go with your instincts – something that is never more true than when working in comedy – with Ferrell reasoning that your gut hope is all you have in comedy, and you forge ahead hoping against hope that people find you funny too. It was during advanced acting classes he discovered that he enjoyed improv comedy. Soon, he began to hone his talent for impersonation – including Hall of Fame baseball announcer Harry Caray – a character he would reprise on *Saturday Night Live* (*SNL*). He also began to create original characters with comedian Chris Kattan – a future Groundling and *SNL* member. They created the Butabi Brothers – two buffoons who go to nightclubs to unsuccessfully pick up women. Sensing momentum in the art of making people laugh, he then decided to ask his dad for advice on giving this 'comedy thing a try'.

Will had seen how a career in the arts had broken up his family, with his dad's busy working schedule seeing him on the road for many months. But his dad surprisingly didn't talk him out of it – instead passing on sage advice that was gained from years of watching talented people never quite earn the success they deserved. He told his son, 'If it wasn't based on luck, I wouldn't worry about it, because you have talent. Just know that there's a lot of luck involved and if you eventually decide to do something else, don't treat it as a failure. Just know it's one-in-a-million.' His father's advice, according to Will, took the pressure off, and he treated his attempt at becoming a comedian as just a game. With his confidence flourishing, he would even take to the stage and attempt stand-up once again, an intimidating battlefield that leaves no room for the weak and has spat out many a would-be comic.

'I wasn't a very good joke writer, but my strength was in setups, premises, and then going into observational humour,' he said (*Port* Magazine, 15.2.2013). 'With stand-up, you're given five minutes, and I'd get maybe two chunks out before my time was up.' His early routine would find him humming the *Star Trek* routine, a quirky set-up that would actually find an audience clapping. He revealed to AintItCoolNews.com: 'Well, I didn't really do that much stand-up. I tried a little, for like a year and a half and maybe did it thirty times. Then I heard about the Groundlings in Los Angeles and I, all at the same time, took classes there all the while doing stand-up and taking acting classes. Then the more I got into the Groundlings programme, stand-up kind of fell by the wayside because it's such a solitary pursuit. It's really exhilarating when it's just you and it's going great, and it's like the worst when it's going bad. Doing sketch and improv with other people is just so much fun. Plus if you fail, at least you're up there with someone. So I had more training in the sketch world to begin with.'

Bolstered by the audience reaction, he tried out, as stated above, for the Groundlings in 1994. The Californian improv and sketch comedy troupe called the Groundlings was founded in 1974. Its name is taken from a line in *Hamlet* – 'to split the ears of the groundlings, who for the most part, are capable of nothing but inexplicable dumb-shows and noise'. On its website it states, 'The Groundlings is an improvisation and sketch comedy theatre that has been entertaining LA audiences for over 36 years. We're a non-profit organisation founded by Gary Austin in 1974. A "Groundling" is one of the 30 company members who write and perform in the theatre's shows and teach classes at the Groundlings School. Our school has been the foremost comedy training ground in Hollywood and the springboard for countless careers. ... Our alumni include Will Ferrell, Kristen Wiig, Phil Hartman, Lisa Kudrow, Paul Reubens, Cheryl Hines, Jon Lovitz, Laraine Newman, Will Forte, Maya Rudolph, Michael McDonald, Kathy Griffin, Phil LaMarr, Cheri Oteri, Chris Kattan, Julia Sweeney, Chris Parnell, Ana Gasteyer and Rachael Harris ... just to name nineteen.'

Describing how the Groundlings came to be, Austin told *The Hollywood Reporter*: 'I was an actor in The Committee in San Francisco. I moved down here, and I was broke. I went to the Hollywood Unemployment Office, where I used to stand in line with Penny Marshall, and I got to the window and the woman said, "Due to a technicality, you are no longer eligible." I panicked and called Howard Storm, who was teaching at the Cellar Theater on Vermont. That was a Thursday. I started teaching on Monday night. Fred Roos, who was the head of feature casting at MGM, gave me 75 names and phone numbers. Tracy Newman, who was my friend, helped me round up a bunch of people from the Comedy Store. So my first night teaching, I had 21 students. I taught for one year, all kinds of people came through. It became kind of a magnet. … We improvised scenes and monologues, and we did scenes from Pinter and Molière and so on. And after a year of doing that, I said, "Let's create a company." We created the Groundlings. I thought of the name. It's from Hamlet's speech to the players.'

Will was accepted into the comedy group, and that was where he discovered that, while there were wittier people with faster improv skills, one thing that could be guaranteed from Will was that he wouldn't hold back. It would be a trademark Ferrell move – the idea that you give everything to a character. He said in a past interview with *Esquire* Magazine: 'It was just funnier to me, and it played funnier, when instead of just yelling at someone in a scene, you're yelling to the point where you're losing your voice – that one extra step. If that's what's called for within the context, isn't that our job as comedians?'

Like most struggling people in the arts, he also had to take other supplementary jobs that he didn't want, being employed as a Mall Santa Claus on one occasion. He told Contactmusic.com, 'I have some experience playing Santa Claus. When we were in the Groundlings together, Chris Kattan was my elf at this outdoor mall in Pasadena for five weeks, passing out candy canes. It was hilarious because little kids couldn't care less about the elf. They just come right to Santa Claus. So by the second weekend, Kattan had dropped the whole affectation he was doing and was like, in the voice of boredom, "Santa's over there, kid."' Will also began working at an auction house thanks to an offer from Viveca Paulin – a friend, who would soon become his wife. It was a job that had its bonuses, particularly for a struggling actor. It meant that he could attend auditions while also taking home a steady pay cheque.

Small roles followed – none of them notable – but they did include roles in TV shows such as *Grade Under Fire* and *Living Single*. There was also the low budget movie *A Bucket of Blood*. The little-seen film was directed by Michael James and starred former Brat Pack star Anthony Michael Hall. The 1995 movie was a remake of the 1959 cult classic by legendary budget producer Roger Corman. The horror comedy focuses on the story of an unpopular busboy who turns to murder to make his macabre sculptures. Ferrell plays a stoner-type character alongside David Cross, another comedian who would land larger roles – most notably as Tobias Funke in the acclaimed show *Arrested Development*. There were also several commercials.

During his time with the Groundlings, Ferrell performed at several venues but had no problem pinpointing his weirdest gig. Former American Football star and *Naked Gun* actor O. J. Simpson was accused of murdering his ex-wife Nicole Simpson and her friend Ronald Goldman in the nineties. Because of Simpson's celebrity status it was always going to be one of the most public trials in history, but given the advent of 24-hour news it suddenly became a worldwide sensation.

While Simpson was finally acquitted, it took over eight

long months before the jury finally got to make their decision. Will told comedian Jeff Garlin for his radio podcast: 'When I was at the Groundlings Theater right down here on Melrose, we were in the show at the time during the O.J. trial. As everyone remembers, the jury was sequestered, they couldn't go anywhere. So we performed for the O.J. jury in a courtroom. We did sketch comedy to 12 people. Which is really hard to do. Sketches didn't have anything to do with court cases, we just did our show. They politely laughed. It was awkward. We were in a brightly lit courtroom in the middle of the day. Sketch comedy for 12 people. But they gave us a standing ovation. That was our public service.'

While there were fun elements, people who made the cut were under no illusion that this would be hard, gruelling work – aided by a ruthless edge. Teacher Jim Rash told Yahoo! Movies: 'There are basically six levels: Basic, Intermediate, Advanced and Improv. And then you move into our Writing Lab series, and if you make it through all those elements, you are asked to join Sunday Company, which is basically our farm team. And you can spend anywhere up to a year and a half in the Sunday Company. And any time during that time, you may or may not be voted into the Main Company.'

Former Groundling and *SNL* star Maya Rudolph told *The Hollywood Reporter*: 'The goal is to work your way into the [Main] Company. When you're standing around in the hallway and you see all the pictures on the wall of the current Main Company members, I would see all these faces that I never saw [at the theatre]. I used to play this game – the people we'd literally never performed with, we'd go, "Get the fuck out, Get the fuck out, Get the fuck out." We're like, "Make room for us, we want to be in the Main Company, you know, get the fuck out, make some room for us kids." Then, my second or third year on *SNL*, I get a call: "Hey, Maya, um, we need some more space in the Main Company, so would you mind stepping down?" I was devastated because I'd worked so hard to get there, but I knew she was right. I'm not there, I get it. I'm literally the creator of Get the Fuck Out. So I got the fuck out.' And former Groundling star Chris Parnell added: 'What is so great about the Groundlings is the process of elimination that happens all the way up the chain. You have got to get that mark of approval at every level. You might be asked to repeat the class, you might be asked to leave. So by the time you make it into the Sunday show, you are guaranteed that people are going to be at a certain skill level, and then in the Main Company, even more so.'

The Groundlings was an excellent comedy apprenticeship for Will. Because of Will's success and countless others, it has been seen as a breeding ground for future *Saturday Night Live* stars. In 2012, for example, five of the Academy Award contenders, including *Bridesmaids* star Melissa McCarthy, original *Bridesmaids* screenwriters Kristen Wiig and Annie Mumolo, and Jim Rash and Nat Faxon, for their adapted screenplay of *The Descendants*, all began at the Groundlings. Comedy star

Jim Rash, who is still a Groundling teacher, told *Entertainment Weekly*: 'There are the people who want the instant gratification ... "When is Lorne [Michaels, *SNL* supremo] going to drop by my class and discover me?" But we try to impress upon people we're not here to teach you how to be funny. I don't care if any of this stuff is funny. I just want to see the story.' The Groundlings was seen by many comedians as a natural stepping stone, like amateur football before trying to make the big leagues. Comedienne Kathy Griffin remembered to *The Hollywood Reporter*: 'The night Lorne came, Lisa Kudrow, Julia Sweeney and I were all auditioning for a spot, and he picked Julia. Lisa and I were crying that night at a diner somewhere. [Later] I was on a little show called *Suddenly Susan* for four years; it changed my life. She became fucking Phoebe [in *Friends*]! We didn't understand there were other things. We all thought it was only about getting on *SNL*.'

She added: 'We had to audition our sketches for one another before they went onstage. And, let me tell you, that's a Michael Vick dogfight right there. So you're with your friends and you guys all love each other, but it's extremely competitive. It's like football. And there are cuts just like football at every single level, and it's all about not getting cut. And then once you don't get cut, trust me, you never get comfortable. Because the weekend Lorne Michaels comes, you want to be picked.' Comedienne Tracy Newman added: 'I think that once the Groundlings became the training ground or a farm company for *Saturday Night Live*, the group dynamic and camaraderie probably disappeared to a certain extent. It became a little bit dog-eat-dog. Even when I was there, it was already starting to be dog-eat-dog.'

While Ferrell would end up performing many years in the famed 30 Rock (30 Rockefeller Plaza, the address of the GE Building which houses the NBC Studios), performing with the Groundlings didn't necessarily mean a future at *SNL* then. He was desperate to become the latest *SNL* member, but it would mean a long audition before he finally got his chance to follow in the footsteps of some of America's most legendary performers.

CHAPTER THREE

LIVE FROM NEW YORK

Will ended up staying with the Groundlings for 18 months. To say his time there was well spent would be an obvious understatement – but his real apprentice-ship was still to be done.

Saturday Night Live is a sketch show with a difference. While it may be almost unrecognisable from its raucous beginnings in the seventies, it's still the show that most comedians are desperate to star in. It was created by Lorne Michaels, and premiered on 11 October 1975, originally titled *NBC's Saturday Night Live*. While the show would be rooted in the audience vaudeville shows, with lots of different talented acts, the atmosphere would be far removed from a family-friendly environment with trained comedians aiming to please an audience with well-worn shtick and crowd-pleasing mainstream routines. While it would arguably become that, when *Saturday Night Live* was introduced, there was one word that could never be levelled at the show – safe. The show introduced a different kind of comedian: supremely talented, but also a rebel. Suddenly, making people laugh became punk and rock 'n' roll – and Saturday nights suddenly became a time to stay in.

It wasn't meant to be like that, however. The show was born purely to ease the workload of US chat-show legend Johnny Carson. The Saturday or Sunday slot was reserved for *The Best of Carson*. However, Johnny Carson demanded that the network stopped showing it at the weekends. He wanted it placed during the week so he could have more time off. It was left to a young twenty-something Canadian called Lorne Michaels to fill the gap. While still nothing more than a rookie producer, he was seen as something of a rising talent. Speaking in the book *Live From New York*, Lorne said, 'So much of what *Saturday Night Live* wanted to be, or I wanted it to be, was cool. Which was something television wasn't, except in a retro way. Not that there weren't cool TV shows, but this was taking the sensibilities that were in music, stage and the movies and bringing them to television.' It would certainly become cool – with a regular roster over the first few years that include Chevy Chase, Dan Aykroyd, the late John Belushi, the late Gilda Radner, Eddie Murphy and Bill Murray – as well as special guests like Steve Martin, the late Andy Kaufman and the late Richard Pryor. It was broadcast from Studio 8H at New York –

and it became THE show to watch. Something that surprised everyone.

Chevy Chase, one of the original members, said in the book: 'I didn't think the show would last more than a year. I'm not even sure Lorne did. We were going to get our kicks in while we could. We went through this stage where basically people tried out with stand-up and [comedy] groups. Gilda [Radner] was already chosen, and Danny [Aykroyd], too. Then [as a head writer] I sat with Lorne in the Steinway building on 57th Street. There was a little proscenium stage, and lots of acts came in. We took Jane [Curtin]. Billy Murray, we didn't take. I don't remember why. But for some reason he didn't make the cut. ... We had our cast and were back at Studio 8H, and there was a little room nearby with a long desk which could act as a stage. Lorne asked everybody to go up there and do something. At the end he said, "Chevy, get up there and do something." So I made up some strange story about Gerald Ford. It was pretty clear that I was a funny guy. I was taller than everybody, and very handsome. It was a good choice, really.'

Despite the success of *Saturday Night Live*, TV was a different breed to what is now. It didn't have shows like *The Sopranos*, *The Wire* or *Breaking Bad* – shows with so much substance that some films pale in comparison to the sheer breadth of character development, ambiguity and nerve-shredding thrills. While *Saturday Night Live* was TV soaked in rock 'n' roll, TV was still the dirty cousin to films, and was a clear stepping stone to the big screen.

So it was no surprise that the lure of the dollars and the chance to become a movie star proved too much for the roster on *SNL*. Chevy Chase was the first one to develop a big-screen career. Others would soon follow suit.

Luckily for Lorne, he had a conveyor belt of talent ready to come off the assembly line to try and achieve their dream of making it big at 30 Rock. Like any enduring show, there have been perceived dips in quality, but every time it looks like the show is coming to an end – and the 'Saturday Night Dead' puns are being dusted off by commentators – up pops a Molly Shannon, a Phil Hartman, an Adam Sandler, a Tina Fey, a Mike Myers, a Bill Hader. You get the point. The show may be a different beast, but talent is talent.

During the season of 1994 and 1995, the show was once again needing that injection of fresh talent. Lorne, apart from a brief period when he left the series in the 1980s, was an ever-present fixture on the show and seemed calm with the knowledge that he would find what it needed. This time, Lorne travelled to Los Angeles to find fresh new talent, and it was there that he met Groundling stars Chris Kattan, Cheri Oteri and Will. Will said to New York Times: 'They came to see us perform at the Groundlings. They were really coming to see Chris. So we all got to choose one piece for the special showcase. I was lucky that two other pieces that I'd written with other cast members were the pieces they chose, so I ended up being in three pieces. If you stopped to really think about it, it was probably pressure-filled, but we were like:

"We're used to performing here. Let's just do our thing." They were really impressed with the show, and they invited myself, Cheri, Chris and Jennifer Coolidge to New York. There wasn't anyone to counsel with.'

One of the stars of *SNL* at the time was Molly Shannon – someone Will knew a little bit. 'I called her up. I think her overriding sense of being a nice person took over, but she said later it was a little weird. "I'm giving you advice, and yet part of me is like, I shouldn't tell you anything."' He also sought advice from a former teacher, telling Backstage.com: 'There was an acting coach here in Hollywood near the Groundlings – Ian Tucker. He did a scene study class on cold reads, and he would literally take scripts from dramas or sitcoms and be like, "You're Kathy, you're Bob. Go." You'd have to read it and listen and react in the moment, and it was so freeing and so interesting, because dramatic scenes would read as comedy all of a sudden, and sometimes comedy scenes would read so dramatic. It was all about being in the moment. And he gave me great advice when I got my *SNL* audition. He said, "Just don't view it as trying to get the job. View it as an experience: a fun trip to New York, a great audition experience. Don't even think beyond that." Which is still hard to do, because you're thinking about the ultimate prize. But I tried to be true to that and not worry about the rest and stay focused on just having it be a cool experience. It took the pressure off, in a weird way.' He added: 'In that first audition we had to do a character of your choice, a political impersonation, if you could do one, and a celebrity impersonation. I did Ted Kennedy doing stand-up comedy. I did the "Get Off the Shed" piece. And I did Harry Caray at a play reading, very much a *Who's Afraid of Virginia Woolf?*-style play.'

Around a dozen new performers were being looked at, but with so many desperate to tread the famed stage it was still a one-in-a-million chance. With so much at stake for Lorne, there wasn't just one audition. Will was first seen at the Groundlings, and then was asked to do a round of auditions. After that there was a call-back round, in which he met Lorne, and then he auditioned again. He went back to the Groundlings, where he was watched once again. Will recounted to *The New York Times*: 'Everyone was camped out in these dressing rooms on the ninth floor. It felt like we were a bunch of paratroopers, about to storm the beach at D-Day. "You hear any news from the front?" You stand outside the stage doors while you're listening to the performer ahead of you finish up. And you're looking along the walls, at all the past cast members. It's just hitting you, and you're trying not to vomit.' Oteri added: 'Chris and Will and I all went out – I don't want to say where, because it's a famous restaurant and it's Italian-owned and I don't want any trouble. But I ended up throwing up all night from food poisoning. All the blood vessels in my eyes were broken, and the blood vessels in my face. I did not sleep. I walked into the audition and the makeup person said, "Oh my God, what happened to you?" I looked like I was in a car accident.'

Meeting Lorne was clearly a nerve-racking prospect for Will – but one in which he was determined to make an impact. Will had recalled an interview with a previous *SNL* star called Adam Sandler, where the funny revealed that he humped a chair like a dog when he met Lorne, and was supposedly hired on the spot. So, his plan was simple. He said in the book Live From New York: 'I thought, "I'm gonna go in there and be funny." I had a briefcase of fake money, and as Lorne starts talking, I was gonna open it and start stacking piles of money on his desk. "Lorne, you can say whatever you want but we all know what really talks. And that's cold, hard cash. Now, I'm gonna walk outta here. You can take the cash if you want. Or not." And then just leave and not come back.'

Will walked into the audition, before soon realising that his plan had a flaw. 'I could tell that the atmosphere was not right for it. Lorne's first thing he said to me was, "OK, so you're funny, you were funny during the first audition. I hope you're funny tomorrow. Because consistency is what we're looking for." I was just like "Oh God." And here's Steve Higgins, who'd been hired the day before, just looking at me. I mean, what comedian walks in with a leather briefcase sitting in their lap? I'm just uncomfortable knowing I have a briefcase full of fake money. Then it was all superseded by asking me what I was going to plan to audition with the following day. The second audition was to be like five minutes of what you want to do on the first show. OK, does that mean stuff that I had done on the first audition that seemed to work, or do you want new stuff? He essentially wanted to see all brand-new stuff, so meanwhile I'm thinking "Oh, my God". So I walked out and they kind of took me through the paces – no, I wouldn't do that, they conveyed to me that they'd seen me do this one thing in the audition and wanted to see if I could cover this other area, and Steve is just looking at me and it's like "Steve, do you have anything you want to ask Will?" And Steve's like "Nice briefcase."' The briefcase stayed unopened during the second audition.

Will added to *The New York Ti*mes, 'I was talking with Chris and Cheri, going, "You guys, I have to literally revamp everything." I was up till three in the morning. And then I did a sketch where I was a guy, alone in my office, who in between taking calls would play with cat toys. There's a point where I'm rolling around on the ground, in complete silence, playing with cat toys. And I'm thinking: "Oh, it's over."' Their next meeting would be two weeks later, with Lorne coming to see him perform at the Groundlings, and then the following week meeting Lorne once again. Will thought the meeting was just another routine one, just another chance for Lorne to see whether Will was right for the job. 'How many times do I have to meet him?' he wondered. So, not knowing that this was in fact a meeting to confirm that he would be getting the job, Will thought this would be a perfect chance to try out his briefcase trick. 'So here I am at the Paramount lot. I was like, "Damn, I got my second chance, I've going to bring my briefcase, I'm going to do the money bit here if I'm ever going to do it." And then, "Lorne's ready to see you – oh, you can just set your briefcase down, don't worry about it." We talked for twenty minutes and then he told me I was hired. And then I walked out, and I just quickly explained to the people outside, "Can you guys just give him some of this fake money? It was this idea I had a long time ago and I never got the chance to do it. That's why I always had this briefcase with me." And then I guess he laughed really hard when he heard the whole thing. I still have the briefcase.'

Will's first sketch gave a taster of what to expect from the comedian. It was a skit based on one of his auditions, and it saw Will play a normal easy-going man hosting a BBQ for his fellow suburban husband. Their idle chit-chat is constantly interrupted by Will screaming at his off-screen children 'Get off the shed!' That seamless transition from a mild manner to sudden bursts of uncontrolled anger was something that Will excelled at.

He was hired for the first nine shows, and was told that he was going to be picked up after that. However, he was only asked for the next six shows. Ferrell recalled in the book *Live From New York*: 'And after that it was whether you were going to be picked up for the next year. And then after that it was year by year, and so you always feel like you're a little bit on shaky ground.' Soon after he arrived, so did a writer who would end up becoming very close to Will. Speaking about Adam McKay: 'We got hired at the same time and became friends right away. Adam became the star writer within a year. Everyone thought he was just amazing. By the second season, he'd been made head writer.'

After he first got hired Will got an apartment and thought he'd best make the most of riding the subway because he believed he would soon be too famous to ride the subway. However, years later he realised he was overreaching his fame. During his first season, he was actually called the 'worst cast member, ever' by some critics. He revealed to *The Guardian* in 2006: 'My friend called with good news and bad news. The good news was that there was this big piece to mark the new *Saturday Night Live* in *Entertainment Weekly* and I was the only member of the new cast mentioned by name. The bad news was that they said I sucked. Big time.' He would soon be credited with its renaissance, though, thanks to his no-holds-barred performances and classic characters like the Boss from Hell, featuring Pierce Brosnan, dead-on impressions of crooner Bob Goulet (an early Ron Burgundy prototype) and George W. Bush. Lorne would eventually say to *People* magazine, 'Will is the glue that holds the show together. He's the first choice of writers for every sketch.'

But Will would still be racked with fears, telling The Guardian: '*SNL* could be brutal, you know. One week you're in five sketches, the next none of them gets in. That was a bad feeling. So it was up to you to come up with your own character and I learnt you had to write it yourself. So I'm used to writing scripts and developing characters for myself, sitting alone and actually thinking and writing. Now I'm learning that method might work and have depth for some characters on film and give the legs for a whole feature to stand. Even so, on set, I'm very much in favour of trying anything without too much thought. I don't like to rehearse or analyse. I'm more, "Let's just shoot it."' Will would later say, '*Saturday Night Live* is such a comedy boot camp in a way, because you get to work with so many different people who came in to host the show and you get thrown into so many situations and learn how to think on your feet.'

One of Will's most famous sketches was 'The Cowbell' sketch, first aired on 8 April 2000. Will Ferrell and other cast members appear as legendary rock band Blue Oyster Cult. Christopher Walken plays rock producer Bruce Dickinson, a cocksure swaggerer of a man who proclaims to the band in the studio that he can work wonders on the new song. The song happens to be 'Don't Fear the Reaper', with fictional member Gene Frenkle played by a bearded Will Ferrell, wildly playing the cowbell in the song. Bruce interrupts the recording, much to the relief of the band, only to find that he wants to hear more cowbell. Will recounted the story on a radio podcast by Jeff Garlin: 'The cowbell in that song is very faint. It's a classic rock song but I would always just hear this cowbell. I would hear it and think "What is that guy like?" Is he like "Hey guys, thanks for letting me play on this one?" Were there arguments that he was playing so loud? "Hey guys, don't fear the reaper was a big hit, maybe I can do another song." That was my idea for the sketch.' Earlier attempts to get the sketch on the show weren't easy, however. While the skit has become something of a legend, it wasn't expected to be a hit.

Said Ferrell: 'What's funny though, was that I had tried out that sketch earlier on that year in the read-through. It went reasonably well. Lorne Michaels was like "Is there a cowbell in that song? Is that something we know? Can we research it?" It didn't get picked, but I held on to it. And later that year Christopher Walken was on, and I dusted it off and I rewrote it for him, and that's why it made it, because of Christopher Walken. Apparently he's now haunted by that sketch.' Christopher Walken said (*Details* Magazine, 20.7.2006): 'I was eating in a restaurant in Singapore, and an Asian couple was at the next table, and the guy turned to me and he said, "Chris, you know what this salad needs?" I said, "What?" He said, "More cowbell." Recently a guy asked me if I would say "More cowbell" on his answering machine. And I did.'

Fallon, who plays the drummer in the skit, also didn't expect it to be the hit it was, revealing to Washington DC's Big 100.3: 'I had just started on the show and I'm not the best actor in the world. I do impressions and stuff like that. So I was stuck in a scene with the great Will Ferrell, who's one of the funniest guys ever and we do the sketch in dress rehearsal and it's OK – it's not even that great. And then, on air ... he came out with a smaller shirt so that his gut would hang out when he banged the cowbell. And everyone just broke up laughing, and I couldn't stop laughing. That's what you get when you play with the big boys.' Even the band itself had to suffer the repercussions of the sketch, with co-founder Buck Dharma admitting to *Vintage Rock*: 'It's funny, that cowbell sketch. We never really thought much about the cowbell, until then. Now, we have to make sure we have the cowbell!'

Another popular recurring role was that of *Jeopardy!* host Alex Trebek. Will told Backstage.com: 'I think it was more that I was watching *Jeopardy!* one night and thought, "Oh, I can kind of do him." So I said, "If anyone wants to write a *Jeopardy!* thing, I can kind of do an Alex Trebek." That's how it started; it wasn't any sort of confidence that it could be popular. They suggested *Celebrity Jeopardy!* and asked Darrell who he'd like to do, and he said, "I've always wanted to do Sean Connery." And it became this total thing.'

In 1998, former *SNL* member Phil Hartman died. he was one of the show's greats, and Will said about the iconic funnyman to AintItCoolNews.com: 'It was good. A lot of times when a comedy person hosts a show, the cast doesn't necessarily get to do all the funny parts, but rather the straight parts that a more dramatic guest might do. I don't remember being in that many sketches with Phil, only a handful, so in a way I kind of feel that I didn't really do that much stuff with him. But just in terms of watching him work and how funny he was, he was a technician in terms of how he went through a sketch and his blocking. It wasn't like, "yeah, let's just wing it" he would really have it down.'

During Will's run, *Saturday Night Live* went back to skewering politics, just like the show did during its golden days, and in doing so gave *SNL* another shot in the arm. Will's take on George W. Bush was soon to be iconic – as masterful as Chevy Chase's impression of Gerald Ford so many years ago. However, it was just pure fortune that he was ever asked to play Bush. Will told Backstage.com: 'In the previous year, prior to the election, I had played Gov. Bush a couple times on *Weekend Update* and things. I think it was Lorne who just said, "Darrell Hammond is going to do Gore. Do you want to do Bush? Because he's tall and you're tall." So I was like, "OK, I'll try it." But I really didn't think he'd get close to winning. And as I watched the campaign through the summer and we started gearing back up to go back for the next season, I was like, "I gotta study this guy; it looks like he's going to be the candidate." Lo and behold, it became a whole thing. At first, it was just kind of a Southern accent. Then we came back and were going to start doing the debates, and I really had to start looking at him. I watched a lot of video on him and tried to piece together whatever I could. I got down the physical posturing of him, in terms of him squinting all the time. And Darrell really helped me, actually. He had some great notes. And it slowly just came along. I'm sure if I went back and watched those early bits, I would see just how far it's come.'

Ratings rose, and suddenly everyone was talking about *Saturday Night Live* again. Even politicians and their advisors had a new show to watch – with Al Gore admitting that they watched *SNL*'s mock performance of his own debate to see where they went wrong. Gore said in a book about *Saturday Night Live*: 'That's true actually. It's not that I set about to use it. It is true though that during the prep for the second debate, somebody brought in the tape – I didn't ask to see it or consciously use it as a tool – but somebody brought it in and said, "You should watch this." And I think it was a way of that person, I can't remember who it was, making a point that the first debate gave grist to the mill for lampooning the sighing and so forth, and that sort of critique that came after the first debate. I think it did have an effect, yes. And I thought it was very funny!'

Will revealed to A.V. Club his thoughts on whether or not he wanted to meet the man that he so wickedly set up: 'You know, there was that stuff written about how the staff loved "strategery", and how he called them "strategery meetings". I had a couple of opportunities to go and meet him, and I declined, partly out of comedic purposes, because when I was on the show at the time, it didn't make sense to really meet the people that you play, for fear of them influencing you. And then the other side of it is, from a political standpoint, I don't want to meet that guy.' Will claimed his fondest memory is of playing George W. Bush opposite Darrell Hammond's Al Gore in the weeks following the contested 2000 presidential election. 'Darrell Hammond and I were like a comedy team all of a sudden, and we really were in a period of time where it was a news event to see what SNL was gonna do that weekend. We did the "Odd Couple" sketch and all these sketches of us being together. We did interviews all week long and the spotlight was on us in a way that was like, "Oh, this must have been what it was like in the 70s, when the show was like the only thing you watched." So, that was like such a cool, cool thing to do, comedically.'

Working on a show like *Saturday Night Live* was more than just a normal gig – it wasn't there just to make people laugh, it was a pop culture event that held a mirror over America. It mined the country's fears for laughs and sought to show that any event, no matter how horrible, could be eased in part by comedy. It was a show that could make America feel safe in the comforting sound of laughter for a brief period on a Saturday night.

Never has that been more true since the events of 9/11. The world seemed to change forever the morning two planes crashed into the twin towers of the World Trade Center, with two other planes hijacked by Islamic terrorists. With a comedy show insignificant due to the devastation caused to the city where the show is held, there was not much thought about getting a comedy fix. There were far too many important issues now, and that New York comedy tradition was very much an afterthought. But for the producers of the show, they had an instant dilemma. With the premiere of the 27th season just 18 days away, they had to gauge the mood of a stricken nation and ask if there was an appetite for humour, particularly satirical slants on current events, something this current troupe excelled at. There was also a worry that any attempt to wring humour out of the situation could be accused of being in poor taste. However, they were urged to go on with the show by then New York Mayor Rudolph Giuliani – who believed that going on with the show would be seen by New Yorkers that it was sign that life must go on. On 29 September 2001, life did indeed go on, with Rudy appearing on the show. In the opening sequence Lorne asked the Mayor was it all right for the show to be funny – with Rudy replying with perfect comedic timing, 'Why start now?'

It was a perfect icebreaker, and it signalled to the country that it was all right to laugh again. Amy Poehler recalled to the authors of *Live From New York*: 'I was home in the East Village on 9/11. I could see the towers out of my window. All of us who were working on the show at the time called each other to see if everybody was OK, and then after all that died down the next question was, "What are we going to do, do we even have a job?" I was thinking they might postpone the show. There was talk about everything coming to a halt. Even thinking about your work, your work in comedy, seemed so kind of frivolous at the time you couldn't even indulge in thinking about it. And then a couple of weeks went by and it was like, "Oh yeah, we gotta put on a show." I just remember it being incredibly emotional and Rudy Giuliani being there. It was very tense and very weird.' Will added in the same book: 'I have a hard time figuring out what the viewpoint of the 9/11 show was. I guess in the final analysis you can't critique it the way you would any other show. Some people said to me, "Great job, it was wonderful" and other people said, "That was lame", because we didn't do really tough sketches. It was a benign show, and maybe that was the best thing to do under the circumstances. The biggest thing I'll take from it was after the show – talking to firemen and policemen. They just kept thanking us and saying "Thanks for the break, we really needed it" and we were going, "What?! We should be thanking you." I did get a little bit emotional towards the end, but I still had my hard hat on.'

Will continued to impress on *Saturday Night Live*, and it seemed to many that he was primed and ready for the big screen.

In 2001, Will was the highest-paid cast member of *Saturday Night Live*, but he left in 2002 to pursue other acting careers. He said to Movies.About.com: 'I just felt I had been on the show for a nice amount of time. I definitely wanted to leave *Saturday Night Live* at a time when I still enjoyed doing the show and so I didn't have a supreme confidence that I would be immediately successful after leaving the show but I just knew it was the right time to test myself and get out there and try other things.' Will said in a 2013 interview with FourEL

Magazine about his time on *Saturday Night Live*: 'You know, *Saturday Night Live* is really … I mean … that was such a unique experience and there's really nothing like it in entertainment, you know? You're doing this weekly live show, you're part of an ensemble and you're working with a major star as the host and you kinda learn to be flexible and adaptable in every situation. And you're used to a certain pace and it's almost an athletic event every week in terms of the hours and things you have to kinda do.'

While he had managed to make his mark on *SNL*, a career in comedy on the big screen was not a sure thing.

CHAPTER FOUR

SHOWING HIS COMEDIC POWER

Will may have been starring weekly on the small screen, but he needed big-screen experience. His chance came in the shape of a former *SNL* member. In 1997, Will made a short if memorable appearance in Mike Myers' movie *Austin Powers: International Man of Mystery*.

A loving homage to the earlier James Bond films, the movie was a hit with critics, but performed modestly at the box office. However, the home video market is where films can find a second life, and soon its success on video gave Myers his chance to make a sequel, and a further third film. The idea was born as a love letter to Myers' childhood, when he would spend hours with his dad watching British comedies with classic actors like Peter Sellers and Alec Guinness. One night, after hockey practice, he started flirting with his wife in an English accent. She started to laugh, and convinced him to make a routine based on the character. It soon led to the creation of Austin Powers.

He said in an interview (*Morning Call*, 6.6.1999): 'I lost my mojo in 1991 when my father passed away. I lost all interest in doing anything, so I took time off. And that's how I came up with Austin Powers, as a tribute to my dad. If my dad had to write a book about life, it would be called *In Praise of Silly*. There were a few things that my father was very vehement about. One thing was "I'm not my job". My dad sold encyclopaedias and memberships to the Better Business Bureau. But he never felt he was his job. And he believed the two most under-rated phrases were "Everything is going to be OK," and "Let's go have some fun." And that's a big thing with my father. You could laugh about anything.'

His father died shortly before the release of *Wayne's World*. Initially, Myers tried to work through his grief. 'My mum was a trained actress [he said in the same inter-view] and she had a show-must-go-on viewpoint. I'll never forget that my dad died on a Thursday and I did *Saturday Night Live* that weekend where I played a young English boy in the bathtub who talks about mummy being with the angels. Life is very weirdly written sometimes. I did that, and it was killing me. Then my dad's funeral was on Monday. And the first screening of *Wayne's World* was on Thursday. Not long after it opened and it was this huge success, I was living in a small apartment in New York and the scripts were literally being shoved under my door. There were agents and fans and paparazzi. And it didn't mean a thing. Not one thing.' After the release of *Wayne's World 2*, which was not as successful as the first film, he began to drop out of the movie business, realising that he had never had time to grieve.

'It was a real "What's it all about, Alfie?" period for me. I came out of it realising how much I love comedy. If we have six people over to our house, I care as much about making them laugh as I do about a big movie. ... I guess you could say I found my mojo again. In this business, you sometimes sit there and stress comes, and [studio executives] want you to do this thing or that thing and you go, "No, I just want to make people laugh." I realised that if you do that, abundance will follow.'

The film begins in 1967, with a colourful British spy named Austin Powers. Spoofing James Bond and the flower-power, Swinging-London vibe, we see Powers battling it out with his arch-nemesis Dr Evil, also played by Myers, against a psychedelic battleground. Evil escapes in a space rocket and cryogenically freezes himself. Fearing that the world won't be able to cope without him when Dr Evil revives himself, Powers volunteers to be cryogenically frozen himself. They both reawaken thirty years later – and both find themselves not suited to the modern climate. Will Ferrell memorably played one of Dr Evil's most trusted henchmen, Mustafa. His fatal mistake was not to prevent Dr Evil's prized pet, Mr Bigglesworth, a white Persian cat, from losing his hair while in suspended hibernation. Sentenced to death by the push of a button, Mustafa is plunged to his apparent fiery death. However, the furnace below doesn't do its job properly, and all through the power of his voice off-screen, Will shines as the anguished Mustafa pleads for help from the man who plunged him to his death, declaring, 'I'm very badly burnt.' Even gunshots from the summoned henchmen don't kill him, with Mustafa shouting, shocked, 'You shot me!'

Acclaimed film critic Roger Ebert said: 'The movie, written by Myers and directed by Jay Roach, is smart enough to know the 1960s are funny without being exaggerated. In one sequence, a fashion photographer shoots 60s fashions, and the clothes, which look like outlandish science-fiction fantasies, are in fact identical to costumes worn during posing sessions in Antonioni's *Blow Up*. Movie buffs will have fun cataloguing all the references to other movies; I clocked *A Hard Day's Night* and *Sgt Pepper's Lonely Hearts Club Band* in addition to *Beyond the Valley of the Dolls* and all the Bond, Matt Helm and *Our Man Flint* references. And, of course, those who remember Bond's adventures with Pussy Galore will be amused by his female antagonist this time, the sinister Alotta Fagina (Fabiana Udenio). ... What is best is the puppy-dog earnestness and enthusiasm that Myers brings to his role. He can only imagine how exciting 1997 will be. Just think: When he was frozen, the world was embracing widespread promiscuity, one-night stands, recreational drugs and mind expansion. He can only imagine what wonderful improvements have come along in the last 30 years.'

Total Film stated: 'Like former *Saturday Night Live* regular Myers' last big film, *Wayne's World*, *Austin Powers* has its faults, mainly that spoofing 007 isn't exactly the cutting edge of satire, and that the end result never stops feeling like a comedy sketch that's been pulled out to 90 minutes. And yet, amazingly, the whole thing is so likeable and done with such utter glee that it's not long before any old crap (a Pussy Galore-alike called Alotta Fagina, for instance) somehow seems hilarious. It's hard to say why *Austin* works when something like *Robin Hood: Men in Tights* so clearly didn't, but it does. Some films seem as if they were a lot of fun to make, but aren't a joy to watch: *Austin Powers* works precisely because you can tell everyone's having a ball.'

The film made a respectable hit at the box office, scoring over $50 million in America, and $70 million worldwide. Nothing to be scoffed at for a movie that only cost just over $16 million to make – but certainly not enough to really contemplate a sequel. The general rule when it comes to sequels – certainly then – was that they cost more and yield less than the film's previous box office takings. So with that train of thought, a sequel would have been a box-office risk. However, the film became a hit on the video market – with positive word of mouth spreading on its home release. It caused such an impact that a sequel was duly made – entitled *The Spy Who Shagged Me*.

In the 1999 *Morning Call* interview, Mike said: 'I have no idea why *Austin Powers* caught on like it did. It's especially bizarre to me that little kids love Austin so much. Jay Roach's theory is that Austin is like Barney. He's happy. He likes to have fun and dance. And the colours are bright. With the first one, we had the attitude of, "Let's scramble and make this small movie." With the second one, it was, "Let's scramble, and keep everybody away, so we can still make a small movie."' Once again, the film was directed by Jay Roach, and starred Mike Myers returning as both Austin and Dr Powers, as well as a brand-new character called Fat Bastard – with Ferrell also reprising his role. The film grossed around $300 million at the box office, smashing the previous film's record.

Myers said: 'I was blown away when the first two films found the audience they did. The only reason we decided to do a third one was to honour the fact that people followed us through one and two. We wrote it from a backwards approach and explained the origins of the worlds of Austin and Dr Evil. It was strangely easy to connect all the stories. It was screenwriting meets Mad Libs.' Roach added: 'It was a little daunting. The success of the second one caught us by surprise a little bit. We had decided not to do even a second one, unless the audience wanted it and we could do something better. And we had to do the same thing here. To top that sequel was quite a task. Mike had a couple of good conceptual humour and character ideas, which got me back into it. Like bringing Austin's father into the film, and the idea of having a third film that seems like the completion of a trilogy. Plus the characters of Goldmember and Foxxy Cleopatra. So there were enough new things that made us think we could pull it off.' In 2011 Roach hinted: 'For me, the secret is Dr Evil ... the Dr Evil world of Mini-Me and the Scott Evil triangle ... I could just watch that forever. So I hope he [Myers] will dig back into that side of it. Austin's a great character, too, but we've done so much Austin, you know, I'd love to go deeper into Dr Evil's world.'

While Will only played a brief part in the films' success, he created a memorable character in minutes. Unfortunately, it would take him several attempts on the big screen before he would have similar impact.

CHAPTER FIVE

TAKING THE LEAD

'**P**eople come up to me and say "I've seen *A Night at the Roxbury* like 20 times!" And I'm like "Really, I'm so sorry."' That is a quote from Will about his first leading-man film.

The film was based on a recurring *Saturday Night Live* sketch, which was certainly not the first skit that has translated from 30 Rock onto the big screen. There have been some successes – most notably *Wayne's World*, so you can see the appeal when there was a chance to bring Will Ferrell and Chris Kattan's Butabi brothers – a pair of night sharks, all flash clothes and nightclub-hopping buffoons trying to score some ladies with usually unsuccessful results. It was a skit that Will and Chris had created when they met each other years ago, but some could see the resemblance to the Wild and Crazy guys – another pair of lovable buffoons who tried, and usually failed, to pick up ladies. They were played by Steve Martin and Dan Ackroyd in early *SNL* skits – with Will noting to Peter T. Chattaway (*The Ubyssey*, 1998): 'I think these guys are – it's hard to actually say this – but in a weird way, they're a little more sophisticated than the wild and crazy guys. Even though they're trying to break into the club world, they still know enough about it to look at least somewhat like they belong, but not really. What else? They live at home. In the same bedroom. That's a difference, too.'

The characters were fairly popular in the series, but it could be argued that the skit's most memorable moment was due to a third Hollywood superstar member. Jim Carrey joined the brothers on the dance floor – or dance floors – for one episode. 'We knew there wasn't any way we could get Jim Carrey to do it with us, and we just thought it would be a cleaner thing if we just kept it to the two guys. I don't think we made any effort to see if Jim was available to do anything in it, and I know he didn't call us.' (*The Ubyssey*, 1998)

The comedy skits were pretty superficial, as many *SNL* sketches are, and they had to flesh them out for the film – to the point where not many even knew that they were brothers. Will told *The Ubyssey*: 'The sketch is pretty much only on one level. It's kind of this physical cartoon, is the best way to describe it. So we just had this blank page that we had to fill from scratch. We just locked ourselves in a room, and between myself and Chris and Steve Koren, who helped us write the sketch, we improvised a lot of it, like how we thought these guys would talk and sound and react and whether or not they're just friends or in the same family. We found that having them in the same family helped to set up that loser mid-twenty-something slacker-who-doesn't-know-what-to-do-with-their-life set-up."

The film was produced by *Clueless* and *Fast Times at Ridgemont High* director Amy Heckerling, with Will crediting her for getting the movie made in the first place. Said Ferrell to *The Ubyssey*: '[Chris and I] didn't necessarily have this in our heads as movie material. But Amy, in particular, identified with these characters or something, so she was like, "What do you think?" And we were like, "Oh, yeah, OK." It wasn't so much that we lobbied for it as that she did, and we were kind of like, "Well, this would be a fun experience and a nice opportunity," so we went forward with it.' Will denied at the time that it's easy going from sketch to cinema – 'Everyone thinks there's some system in place, like a Turning Sketches Into Movies Department on the show, but there really isn't a science to how it's done,' he says. 'Like I said, our thing happened because Amy Heckerling sparked interest in it. I think it's a weird thing, I think there's no real rule to the way some sketches become movies and others don't, and I think it's OK if you don't feel the need to turn it into a movie.'

And Will conceded (in *The Ubyssey*, 1998) that the failure of other *SNL* sketches on the big screen weighed heavily on his mind: 'Yeah, of course it did. That was definitely something that we thought about. And yet, in a way, there's no guarantee with a movie that *anyone* makes, and we felt that this was a little different situation in that we had Amy Heckerling produce, and this cast is different too, in the sense that everything is approached more from comedic acting as opposed to the world of stand-up, which is more joke-conscious. We're more character-driven, and I think that lends itself to better moviemaking.'

The seeds of the Roxbury guys began years before when Chris and Will were at a Los Angeles club and spotted one guy leaning against the bar. Ferrell recalled in an interview during a junket for the film: 'He was dying to be part of the scene, but he'd try and try, and come up with nothing. He was really out of his element – a dorky fish in glitzy water.'

The movie was filmed in Los Angeles, achieving the city's authentic atmosphere by shooting at popular night spots, including the Mayan Club and several places on the Sunset strip. It was the Mayan Club which was used to represent the titular club. A lavish theatre in the 1920s, it was then converted into a party spot. The film's costume designer was Mona May, who kitted the boys out in a combination of Euro-chic and American cool, with up-to-the-minute creations from designers such as Chanel, Gucci, Versace, Matsuda, Calvin Klein and Tommy Hilfiger. Will said, 'Technically, what the brothers wear is hip clothing, très high fashion. They're totally into the clothes they see in magazines. The trouble is, it looks great on models, but on them it's totally cheesy.'

It was clear that Will was ready for Hollywood stardom, but *A Night at the Roxbury* was not the right movie. Roger Ebert noted: 'A *Night at the Roxbury* probably never had a shot at being funny anyway, but I don't think it planned to be pathetic. It's the first comedy I've attended where you feel that to laugh would be cruel to the characters.' And he wasn't the only critic to have similar thoughts. It scored a paltry 11 per cent on Rotten Tomatoes. *Empire* magazine blasted: 'Even at just 82 minutes *A Night at the Roxbury* seems like an hour-and-a-half too long. And *Sight and Sound* magazine stated that it was 'profoundly unfunny'. *Variety* magazine also panned the film, but at least stated: 'Uninspired screenplay never lifts this into the high silliness that the *Wayne's World* movies managed, but the overall effect is painless enough.'

Will told MovieHole in 2003: 'It's a strange thing that one. It wasn't a hit at the cinemas, it wasn't a flop either. But it found more of a life on video and DVD. I was in New York, and this foreign cab driver turns and looks at me and goes, "Roxbury guy! I love it."' Will also hinted that he wasn't such a big fan of the movie, saying: 'Let's just say I liked my part in *The Ladies Man* [another *SNL*-inspired flick] better than I liked the whole *Roxbury* movie. I couldn't believe it when Lorne Michaels said he wanted to make a movie about the *Roxbury* guys. So no sequel, I've kind of done that.'

It took around $30 million at the bank office, which wasn't an abject failure – but for his first film as a leading man it wasn't the breakout success for Ferrell that he may have wished for. That would be another film. Until then, he would have to be satisfied with still starring in *Saturday Night Live* and filming supporting appearances in movies.

CHAPTER SIX

LENDING A SUPPORTING HAND

In 1999, Will appeared in *The Superstar* – another attempt at bringing an *SNL* sketch to the big screen. This time the spin-off was based on a socially inept girl called Mary and her life at a Roman Catholic private school. She is a social outcast, but is someone who is desperate to be popular so she can get a kiss from Sky Corrigan – played by Will Ferrell.

The character was created and played by Molly Shannon, and had appeared in several *SNL* skits. She told Cinema Review: 'I was doing my first comedy show and we were doing this improvisation exercise to develop characters for the show called "through the door": you go through the door, you shake hands, you introduce yourself and you're a character. Well, I just went through the door and became Mary Katherine Gallagher, this nervous girl who shook hands a lot and didn't know when to stop shaking.' The character made her *SNL* debut at the end of 1995, shocking an Irish priest, played by Gabriel Byrne, by lifting her leg during a school talent-show audition and flashing her white cotton underpants. Ferrell remembered the sketch, telling Cinema Review: 'It was truly a magical moment because it was the first time that anyone in this [current] cast had done something which caused the audience to erupt. They were going crazy, Molly just killed, destroyed them. It was very impressive.'

It was rare for a female-dominated *SNL* sketch to be given a chance at a movie, and even Molly was cautious when approached to make the movie. She said in Cinema Review: 'When Lorne Michaels came to me and asked me to do this movie I was really excited. But then I got really scared because I don't think that every character that does well on *SNL* should be in a movie. I called my friend, Steve Koren, who's written a lot of the sketches with me. I thought if we could come up with a good story, this could work. I never doubted that the character had enough dimension to sustain and deserve a whole feature-length story. In my head, I knew she was more than a character that sniffs her armpits and falls down and does that all that wackiness.'

Remarking about the transition from *SNL* to movies, she revealed: 'It's definitely, at times, been hard. And I think that I didn't really understand how the movies worked, and I think I thought it was easier than it was, and I was like, "Oh God, this is hard." So I kind of had to go through like a grieving process of what I thought maybe the movie industry was. And I think Tina Fey said a great thing on NPR [national public radio] where she said Hollywood is a lot harder on women than *SNL*. Because people would always be like, "Oh, *SNL*'s so hard on women." And she was like, "I think Hollywood's a lot harder on women than *Saturday Night Live*." You know? But I think … I don't mind struggling because sometimes I feel like it can help you create something that you might not have thought of through that struggle where you get like, "God, it's not so easy." But then you're forced to get together with a friend, or … Usually, something comes out of that struggle, so that's kind of the way I look at it. I try not to blame anyone. You know, people are just going to write what they know. It was like that at *Saturday Night Live*. Like you could go, "Why aren't those boys writing for me? Why are they just writing sketches with bears and robots? Why can't they write a complicated female part?" They don't mean any harm, they just want to write about bears and robots, you know? So if you want to do something for yourself, you have to create that for yourself, you know? And so Hollywood's similar in that once in a while, you're so lucky. Well, Mike White, this is a special circumstance, but I feel like, "Wow, how lucky." I just feel gratitude because I know how hard it is, you know.'

Like *A Night at the Roxbury*, *Superstar* wasn't that successful. The film scored a lowly 32 per cent at Rotten

Tomatoes, with many critics slating the latest *SNL* silver-screen adaptation. *The Globe and Mail* said: 'A stick-figure Rembrandt that provides neither the quick surreal poke of a TV satire nor the full lustre of an actual movie', while the *Chicago Tribune* stated that it was 'synonymous with crap'. Not all were left unimpressed, with *Variety* calling it a 'pleasant surprise'. The review added: 'Steven Wayne Koren's screenplay drop-kicks entertaining spoofs of *Armageddon* and *Carrie*, as well as funny musical numbers amid the well-tuned, slapsticky high school satire. Invention flags somewhat after the halfway point, but rallies for Mary Katherine's climactic talent show extravaganza and some good closing gags.' With a budget reported to be around $34 million, the film only recouped $30 million of that at the US box office. While it would have made that deficit back at the worldwide box office and on home video sales, it would still have been deemed disappointing by the studio.

Will next starred in *Dick*, a winning and warm American comedy about two teenage girls, played by *Dawson's Creek* star Michelle Williams and Kirsten Dunst, who end up becoming the infamous Deep Throat – the legendary and mysterious source who brought down US President Richard Nixon following the Watergate scandal. The fictional coming-of-age story was well played by the two leads, and Will gave it an extra spark in the role of Bob Woodward, one of the journalists who broke the famous story.

Dick scored an impressive 70 per cent on Rotten

Tomatoes, with *Variety* stating: 'The best and certainly most amusing theory yet advanced for the identity of Deep Throat is put forward by *Dick*. This audacious, imaginative political comedy will have Watergate buffs in particular, and baby boomers in general, laughing loud and long. But Andrew Fleming's sharp-witted pic appears to occupy the same niche as the recent *Election* in that it's a devilishly clever satire about teenagers that, para-doxically, will appeal much more to critics and sophisticated older auds than it will to teens themselves, who, in this case, will surely find many of the Watergate refs flying right over their heads. Sony release is sure to find an ardent, if modest-sized, following, one that could expand considerably down the line in video and other ancillary markets.' Roger Ebert called it a 'bright and sassy comedy' – while *Entertainment Weekly* stated: 'Twist follows nutty twist – and never more gleefully than when the girls tangle with *Washington Post* reporters Bob Woodward (Will Ferrell) and Carl Bernstein (Bruce McCulloch). Any residual lustre left on the famous journalists so many years after *All the President's Men* is casually scrubbed off in a definitive bit of historical revisionism as the two ("muckraking bastards" Nixon calls them) are indelibly portrayed as vain, obnoxious wonks whose luck really turned when they met Betsy and Arlene, unnamed sources.'

Despite a smattering of bad reviews – 'the film gets off on the wrong foot and never recovers' – *Dick* was brightly received by critics. However, it was poorly received by audiences and only raked in $6 million at the box office. A reason for the disappointing box office could be the poor marketing of the movie, with the film aimed at teenagers, when perhaps it should have been aimed at older audiences, given the seventies period and the film's brazen retelling of a famous incident.

In August 2000, Ferrell married Viveca Paulin, his long-time Swedish girlfriend. They had met in an acting class in 1994. They have three sons – the oldest is Magnus, who was born on 7 March 2004. Their second son, Mattias, was born on 30 December 2006, and Axel was born on 30 January 2010.

While his personal life was on solid ground, he was still trying to find THAT part. But Will always knew that success on *Saturday Night Live* didn't necessarily mean instant success. All he had was his belief that he had what it takes. He told IGN: 'Why have some gone on to bigger and better things? *Saturday Night Live* is such a specific thing. But you do have to be given the right opportunities and then have the capabilities within yourself to take advantage of them. And you have to be able to develop material that's closer to your sensibility. I think those factors increase your chance for success. They don't guarantee them, by any means. It is a crapshoot, though.'

Will next starred in yet another *Saturday Night Live* adaptation. This time the film was based on a sketch starring Tim Meadows as the titular Ladies Man – a smooth-talking broadcaster who offers romantic advice, usually of the dubious kind. It would be the last *SNL* production of a sketch show turned to silver screen for years, following a yet another box-office disappointment. It scored a mere 11 per cent on Rotten Tomatoes. Roger Ebert blasted: '*The Ladies Man* is yet another desperately unfunny feature-length spin-off from *Saturday Night Live*, a TV show that would not survive on local access if it were as bad as most of the movies it inspires. There have been good *SNL* movies, like *Wayne's World*, *The Blues Brothers* and *Stuart Saves His Family*. They all have one thing in common: *SNL* producer Lorne Michaels was not primarily responsible for them. Michaels had nothing to do with *Stuart* and *Blues Bro*thers. Credit for the glories of the *Wayne's World* pictures, which he did produce, should arguably go to their directors and stars. Mike Myers went on to *Austin Powers*. Michaels went on to *Coneheads*, *Superstar*, *A Night at the Roxbury*, and now *The Ladies Man*. If I were a Hollywood executive, I would automatically turn down any Michaels *SNL* project on the reasonable grounds that apart from the Mike Myers movies, he has never made a good one. He doesn't even come close. His average star rating for the last four titles is 1.125. Just to put things in perspective, the last three Pauly Shore movies I reviewed scored 1.5.'

Entertainment Weekly stated: 'If *The Ladies Man* had plopped Leon into a tiger-striped night world as casually raunchy as he is, he might have emerged as a kind of funk soul brother to Austin Powers. This, however, is one more case of a winning *SNL* character tamed by the wan, fizzled farce around him. There's an amusingly gross soul food eating showdown, as well as an overemphatic turn by Will Ferrell as a repressed gay wrestling fanatic who wants to castrate Leon. By the end, the movie has done it for him.' And the website Common Sense Media stated: 'First, the good news: *The Ladies Man* isn't very long, and it's not as bad as some of the other *SNL* movies, like *Superstar* and *It's Pat*. There are some very funny moments, and Will Ferrell is great as the husband of one of The Ladies Man's ladies and some of the other *SNL* and *Kids in the Hall* veterans provide some bright spots. And, it's always great to see Billy Dee Williams. Now, the bad news. You can't make a five-minute *SNL* sketch into a feature-length movie, even a short one. It will have to have stretches of obvious padding, which this flick has.'

While Will seemed confident on the big screen, his wild energy hadn't been tapped properly, nor had he successfully moved away from the shackles of his TV roots. He was still on *SNL* at this point and the movies, *Austin Powers* aside, had done little to move him away from the show onto the big screen. Help was at hand from Ben Stiller. The funnyman actor directed, co-wrote and starred in *Zoolander*, a hilarious satire on the model industry. Dim-witted supermodel Derek Zoolander, played with star-making effect by Stiller, is one of the biggest supermodels in the world and is coveted by the fashion world. However, he fears his stardom is on the wane thanks to the introduction of a rival male supermodel – played with cocksure swagger by Owen Wilson. Ferrell plays the film's nemesis, fashion mogul

Jacobim Mugatu, who is summoned by the fashion industry leaders to find a gormless model who could be brainwashed easily into killing the new prime minister of Malaysia – a progressive leader who wants to stop cheap child labour in his country. Derek Zoolander is brainwashed to perform the murder.

The plot was described thus: 'Derek Zoolander's world is knocked off its axis when, anticipating his victory of a fourth straight Male Model of the Year Award, it is instead handed to the dashing hot newcomer, Hansel (Owen Wilson). Facing the devastating reality that he is no longer the world's number one supermodel, Derek searches for a purpose in life and returns to his southern New Jersey roots to work in the coal mines with his father and brothers. Unfortunately, Derek's blue collar father (Jon Voight) is none too pleased to see him, given the shame he feels concerning his son's unmanly profession. Rebuffed by his family, Derek returns to Manhattan where the now ubiquitous Hansel is more than he can take. The two stars engage in a modelling "walk-off" to determine once and for all the best runway talent, from which a mutual respect ultimately develops.'

Dressed in outlandish costumes, and an even crazier hairstyle, Mugatu was a perfect comedy creation, and brilliantly tailored for someone of Will Ferrell's talents. Ferrell said about his look to Cinema Review: 'Mugatu likes to wear corsets, which were real ones I had to squeeze into. It was insane. Once we stopped shooting, I was addicted to wearing corsets. The big bold decision though, was to dye my hair platinum blonde, no less than three times, as you'll see. A lot of people thought it was a wig. We created this crazy hairstyle and I couldn't cut it. So, half the season of *Saturday Night Live*, I had to wear wigs to cover this big head of platinum hair. Total insanity.'

The film, while sometimes uneven, is a comedy delight, with Will's forceful turn as the villain a perfect foil for the gormless comedy duo. While Will was becoming a big hit on US small screens, *Saturday Night Live* doesn't have quite the same grab worldwide, so *Zoolander* was the first real hint of his talent in the international arena. His turn in *Austin Powers* was nothing more than a cameo, but in *Zoolander* you really felt his comedic prowess. So for many people this was the first real sight of Will at his very best. His manic delivery and his composed screen presence finally delivered his big-screen promise.

While reviews were mixed, it was clear this was a wholly original comedy. The BBC said: 'Ben Stiller's third directorial outing is an extremely silly and soft-centred satire on the fashion industry. Firmly in the tradition of the big screen outings of US TV comedy *Saturday Night Live* – of which Stiller is a graduate – it's patchy and occasionally irritating. However, it's also occasionally very funny.' *Empire* magazine noted the rising talent of Will: 'Some actors practically guarantee quality: Kevin Spacey, for example (we'll ignore *Pay It Forward*, as indeed everyone should). Inversely, Chris Klein's name above the title is ominous indeed. Meanwhile, Will Ferrell is fast becoming a byword for patchy but funny all-star spoofs. This month alone, he overacts wildly in *Jay and Silent Bob Strike Back*, and again here as the flamboyant fashion designer criminal mastermind, Mugatu. The message is clear: if you see Ferrell, stick around.' *Variety* commented: 'Profoundly silly but sporadically entertaining, Ben Stiller's *Zoolander* is an extremely slight and goofy farce of the fashion industry, this time around targeting male rather than female models. Based on the character that Stiller and MTV Movie Awards writer/producer Drake Sather created for the 1996 VH1/Vogue Fashion awards, the new comedy, which might have been inspired by Mike Myers' far superior *Austin Powers*, is still essentially a short, strenuously stretched to the limits of feature-length.'

The film was released just three weeks after 11 September 2001, and it did not tickle the funnybone of late film critic Roger Ebert. In one of his most scathing reviews, Ebert stated: 'There have been articles lately asking why the United States is so hated in some parts of the world. As this week's Exhibit A from Hollywood, I offer *Zoolander*, a comedy about a plot to assassinate the prime minister of Malaysia because of his opposition to child labur. You might want to read that sentence twice. The logic: Child labour is necessary to the economic health of the fashion industry, and so its opponents must be eliminated. Ben Stiller stars as Derek Zoolander, a moronic male model who is brainwashed to perform the murder. Didn't it strike anybody connected with this movie that it was in bad taste to name a real country with a real prime minister? A serious political drama would be one thing, but why take such an offensive shot in a silly comedy? To some degree, *Zoolander* is a victim of bad timing, although I suspect I would have found the assassination angle equally tasteless before Sept. 11.' However, Stiller later revealed that Ebert afterwards apologised for his scathing comment. He recounted: 'To his credit, I ran into him like five or six years later backstage at *The Tonight Show*. He said, "Hey, I just want to apologise to you. I wrote that about *Zoolander*, and I [now] think it's really funny. Everything was a little crazy back then. It was Sept. 11 and I went overboard."'

The film took over $40 million, and it certainly wasn't a huge hit at the box office. But like *Austin Powers*, *Zoolander* was a film that had its life breathed back on the home video market. It became cult viewing thanks to its hugely quotable lines, crazy characters and funny interplay between Stiller, Wilson and Ferrell. A sequel has long since been mooted. Stiller teased some plot details in 2011, saying: 'Ten years is a thousand years [in the modelling industry]. They're both totally out of it and have to start from scratch. And then there are things set up at the end of the first movie that we're able to build on, like Derek and Matilda have a son, and Mugatu went to jail. There's a lot there, I'm excited about the idea of doing it. It feels like it's getting close to going.' He also added: 'Will Ferrell is written into the script and he's expressed interest in doing it. I think Mugatu is an integral part of the *Zoolander* story, so yes, he features in a big way.' But in 2012 Stiller said: 'We have a script, as we've had for a little while, and it's not quite coming together right now, but I hope it does. I would like to do it at some point in the future.'

Will would play another manic bad guy in *Jay and Silent Bob Strike Back*. Written, directed and starring Kevin Smith, it was the fifth film that was set in Smith's 'View Askewniverse' – a universe he first started in *Clerks*. *Clerks* was a 1994 comedy that propelled Smith into superstardom. The black-and-white independent movie was shot for a paltry $27,500, and was funded by Smith's maxed-out credit card. Shot in a store, it followed the adventure of two clerks and their mindless conversations over a day in their lives. Featuring whipper-snapping pop-culture dialogue, playfully lewd references and hilarious exchanges, Smith was seen as one of the indie kings. His follow-up *Mallrats* was something of critical flop, but his stock rose again with the wonderfully observed *Chasing Amy*, a drama about a man who falls in love with a lesbian. Smith's controversial religious road movie *Dogma* ruffled some feathers, and for his next movie he decided to make an out-and-out comedy featuring his regular characters Jay and Silent Bob – the latter played by Smith.

When he was asked to star in the movie, Will researched Smith's output, telling AintItCoolNews.com: 'I had seen *Chasing Amy* and really liked it and then renting the rest of his films and literally sitting down one night and watching all of them, and obviously became more attuned to what he does. I mean I had a general sense of Kevin Smith – his type of work, his movies and his style. I absolutely loved *Dogma*. I also saw his progression as a filmmaker too and that was fun to see for me.' Will added: 'I know *Dogma* got critical acclaim and yet I heard some people say, "Oh, it's not as good as *Mallrats*," but in a way I think it's his best movie. So in answer to your original question – yeah, for the most part familiar and then I really wanted to dig my teeth into getting to really know his work and when I did, I was like "Wow! this would be so much fun to do."' One of the things that appealed to Will was making an adult comedy, noting: 'It's obviously a radical departure from some of the *Saturday Night Live* films I've gotten to work on, which are pretty much characters from the show. You know what you're gonna get with it – very much in that PG13 realm of "safe family" comedies. I mean we get to do some crazy stuff too, but we're always dealing with the censors. But to get to work on something like this in which you can just kind of go for it – it's such a blast. Like a new-found adolescence.'

He added: 'I'm really still learning about film in some ways because obviously you don't have that audience right in front of you. Doing comedy on a show like *SNL*, you get the immediate feedback as to whether or not something's working. So it's easier in that regard. On film, it's more like you have to learn to trust your own instincts to hang in there. Films are a real tricky thing.

I've had times when no one's really laughing, including the crew.'

In *Jay and Silent Bob Strike Back* Ferrell plays Federal Wildlife Marshal Willenholly, a bumbling, buffoon version of Tommy Lee Jones's grizzled turn as the Federal Marshal in *The Fugitive*. Will said about the character to AintItCoolNews.com: 'He wants to have the same respect and tries to conduct himself with the same bravado and as often is the case his information is wrong and no one respects him and he gets a little frustrated. He's the guy who tried to get into the FBI and couldn't make it so he became a wildlife marshal. That was the second best thing he could think of.'

While Smith wrote the film, and is known for his sharp comedy writing, he allows his actors freedom in improvising – well, certainly in Will's case. When Smith was asked why he allowed Ferrell lots of freedom to ad lib but wasn't as generous to Affleck in *Mallrats*, Smith joked to Hollywood.com: 'Well, the difference between Will Ferrell and Affleck improvising is Will Ferrell is very funny.' Will said about the process: to AintItCool.com 'Usually if I have an idea I'll be like, "Hey, what if we changed it up this way?" And he'd be like, "Oh, OK. Let's try that." And then sometimes I'll just do it on my own and to be frank, he's not very happy with it. He'll banish me for an hour and a half. He'll put me in a time out. I'll have to sit in this special solitary confinement box on the set.' He added: 'We pretty much see eye to eye in this character. Also, he told me he wrote it with me in mind in terms of my delivery and that sort of thing. It's material that's right up my alley, so yeah, we totally share the same sense of humour.'

Will called the film 'a fantastic experience all around!' It made $30 million domestically, and was met with average reviews from most critics. *Empire* magazine stated: '*Strike Back* is an infuriatingly patchy experience, with moments of inspired foulness. Jay's rant in support of the "Coalition for the Liberation of Itinerant Tree-dwellers" (work it out for yourself) is a highlight, as is Chris Rock's angry, black film director ('They stole *Sesame Street* from me – I was going to call it *Niggas Wid Puppets*!'). But the gag hit/miss ratio is really only about 50/50 and the rambling, freewheeling plot is virtually non-existent at points. In the end, it's a kind of stoner *Road To …* movie, with considerably more references to bitch-slapping than was usual in the Hope/Crosby franchise.'

Will had filmed several supporting appearances while still working on *Saturday Night Live*, but when he made the decision to leave the show in 2002 it was because of the knowledge that he had a couple of roles up his sleeve, both wildly different, but were sure to give that big-screen break. He told All In Movie: 'When I think back, *Old School* was in the can, but they'd actually pushed the release from November to February of 2003, which usually signals that there's trouble. And then there was a small conversation about this script called *Elf* that sounded like a really funny premise, but I read the script and thought: "Oh, we'll probably have to work on this a bunch." So those were my prospects, you know. That was it.'

What Will didn't know was just how much Frank the Tank was going to explode on the big screen.

CHAPTER SEVEN

THE NEW CLASS

Back in the early days of *Saturday Night Live*, the movies that came out featuring the stars were raucous affairs like *Animal House*, *The Blues Brothers* and *Caddyshack* – the latter famous for its legendary off-set exploits. The film, on- and off-screen, was filled with madness, and director Todd Phillips was eager to bring that sense of anarchy back to a new audience.

The film would be called *Old School*, and would focus on a trio of men all looking for a new adventure. Vince Vaughn's character Beanie is desperate for the fun of his youth and eager for a temporary sanctuary away from his wife and kid. Luke Wilson's character Mitch is still reeling from finding out his wife is a serial adulterer, and then there's Will Ferrell's character, Frank, a man who has transformed from his wild partying ways and crazy alter ego, Frank the Tank, into a respectable man, thanks mainly to his new bride. However, when Mitch finds himself new accommodation right next to a college campus, his friends decide to make it a new fraternity. High jinks rightly ensue, and it forms one of the most distinctive and influential comedies of the millennium.

It was brought together by Todd Phillips, who had already made an award-winning documentary entitled *Frat House*. The idea of *Old School* was one that excited him. He said in the film's production notes: 'These aren't college kids. These are three guys in their thirties who are at that point in their lives when they have to choose what path they're going to take. In a nutshell, it's responsibility versus irresponsibility. So they take what most people would consider to be a step backwards and devolve over the course of the story, but it ends up being to their advantage.' Phillips added: 'The genesis of this film was inspired by a friend of mine in the advertising industry named Court Crandall. He loved *Frat House*, and one day he said to me, "You know what would be funny is a movie about older guys who start a fraternity of their own." I told him he should write it, and he came back with a loose version of what eventually became *Old School*.'

The film's executive producer was Ivan Reitman – a comedy veteran, and one who was well versed in working with *Saturday Night Live* stars, including directorial work on *Ghostbusters* with Dan Ackroyd and Bill Murray, and the king of Frat-house comedies, *Animal*

House, which starred *SNL* legend Jim Belushi. 'Ivan is amazing,' said Todd. 'He really knows plot structure and character development and all the nuts and bolts of writing a great comedy that I am, frankly, still learning. He's just on top of it.' In the film's production notes, Reitman recalled: 'There are only so many original college-based movies you can do, and I thought there was a funny movie to be made out of these three good friends who each come to a crisis point at about the same moment in their lives, and their solution is to start a fraternity – the fact that they are long gone out of college notwithstanding. I thought that if we could capture that transitional moment when you have to make the decision to mature into full adulthood, it would be something audiences could relate to.' Phillips added: 'These guys are in their 30s and out of step with college kids today, but they want so badly to fit in again, each for different reasons. *Old School* is about their usually left-footed attempts to recapture those times. Maybe because I'm 31 and sort of at that same point, it was a topic I felt was fun and interesting to explore.'

Talking about the casting, Phillips said: 'Vince was the guy I wanted from day one. I think he's one of the funniest actors around, which has gone pretty much untapped, at least in the mainstream. Once we had Vince, I thought it would be amazing if we could get Will and Luke, and it all just fell into place. I feel very lucky. These guys all come from different places and their comedy is different, too, but the chemistry was just perfect.' Reitman added: 'There is something in their energies that mixes together to create something that's delicious to watch. The cockiness of Vince Vaughn is a perfect foil to the kind of innocence of Will Ferrell. And then you have Luke Wilson, God bless him, who is right down the middle and is the glue that holds this unusual ensemble together.'

Ferrell talked in the film's production notes about what attracted him about the role: 'Number one, I wanted to be able to run naked through the streets of Montrose. Once I found a role that satisfied that, I knew I was OK. Actually the opportunity to work with Vince Vaughn and Luke Wilson was the biggest thing for me. Then I met Todd Phillips and thought that the combination of the four of us working together, along with the premise of the movie, had the potential for a really fun comedy.'

Each of the trio brought a different comedic dynamic to the movie, with Ferrell mastering the over-the-top physical humour, Vince Vaughn perfecting the sarcastic Bill Murrayesque persona and Luke Wilson mastering the deadpan, sarcastic humour. Talking about the improv on the shoot, Luke added to About.Movies.Com: 'You get a good script and then when you get somebody like Todd [Phillips] who wrote it, and that helps, and that he's directing it. Then, of course, Will and Vince would come up with really good ideas so it's fun to be able to show up on the set. It's like you're blocking out a scene or trying to figure out how you're going to do it physically and where everybody is going to stand. Then, you start getting ideas. Not all the time, but a lot of times you get an idea of something to add. Especially with a comedy, you've got the clear-cut goal of trying to make a scene funny. It's not like drama where you're trying to achieve some kind of emotion or trying to further the story along. You're trying to figure out what's the funniest way to do something. So then, yeah, you do end up trying to improvise.'

What Ferrell brought to the screen, previously untapped in his performances on screen, was his vulnerability. He could play brash, and in the character of Frank, most notably his party-going alter ego Frank the Tank, he was a force on the silver screen. But it was the quieter moments that Will imbued in this character that gave Frank, and indeed the film its heart. Will said to Movies.About.com: 'I definitely think that's what this movie brings [that's] a little different than what you think you're going to see. It's kind of what attracted the three of us to the material in the first place. There was a little more behind the characters than just going from one funny scene to the other.' Vince Vaughn added to the same website: 'I started in Chicago at the Improv Olympic, which is live improv and team improv. The first thing that I did that started things off was with Favreau and *Swingers*, which was a comedy but a character-driven comedy. I prefer that kind of comedy. Then we did *Made*, which is a darker, smaller, character comedy. [After *Swingers*] I got offered mostly comedies but I chose not to do them because I didn't really think they were funny. I find the things that make me laugh are over-commitment to a very real thing, not just falling down for falling down's sake. That's why I'm a fan of Will's work because even with a broad comedy, he's very much in his circumstances and there's a lot of truth there.'

One of the film's biggest highlights was the scene where Frank the Tank runs down the street naked, much to his shock of his new wife who just happens to drive by. Ferrell said about the scene: 'The fact that this character, that his streaking was kind of a result of falling off the wagon, the fact that it made sense was the reason why I was really into doing it, and was why I was able to commit on such a level. If it was just for the sake of getting a crazy shot, then I don't think it makes sense.' Wilson joked about Ferrell's bare-faced spirit for the scene, saying: 'Well, I know Will flew in his acting coach from Kentucky, Jimmy Beam, that night.' The scene was extra nerve-racking for Will, as he had to perform the nude scene in front of rapper Snoop Dogg. Will remarked: 'Snoopy, as I like to call him. That was probably more intimidating because we shot that the very last day of shooting, so I'd already done the streaking part by myself. But to actually be in front of Snoop Dogg that close naked, that was more intimidating than anything.'

Snoop has a cameo in the film, playing himself as a special guest appearance at the first party of the new frat house. Phillips offered the Snoop the part of Huggy Bear in his upcoming adaptation of *Starsky & Hutch*, but only if he made the short appearance in *Old School*. Phillips said of the cameo in the film's production notes: 'That was done through bribery. If you remember the TV show … Huggy Bear was this street informant, sort of a pimp. And you never knew what he did but he was kind of like a snitch. So all these guys, all these great African-American actors, really wanted to be Huggy Bear because they grew up like I did on the show, and he was the coolest guy on TV. So I know Snoop wanted it … and out of respect I had to go to him first anyway because he is the coolest guy in the world. So when I went to him I said, "I want you to do Huggy Bear," he was really excited. And I said, "Oh yeah, also will you do this little thing for me in *Old School*, a little cameo?" So he kind of had to do it I think.'

Vince said about working with Snoop: 'They knocked on my door and said, 'Snoop Dogg's a big fan and he wants you to come, hang out, and play video games.' It was the last day of shooting and [it was] the party scene with no real dialogue except one scene that me and Snoop shot that wasn't in the movie. [My friends and I] went in there and just had a good time and played video games and laughed and hung out for a while. I came out and saw Luke; he was watching the news. He was like, "No one told me everyone was in Snoop's trailer."'

The film works because of the easy-going chemistry of the leads, and, just by listening to the film commentary, you can tell that the banter was replicated on and off screen. Luke added: 'We kept having this phrase like,

"Let's shoot this movie 70s style. Come on, it's us three, let's have fun." We got caught up in how well-behaved we were all the time. Really we were, and we never did manage to go "70s style" but that was our mantra throughout the whole movie. "Let's get 70s style." But we never really did do it.' Vince Vaughn remarked: 'We had a lot of fun and were always joking around with each other. We call ourselves "The Wolfpack" because we always turn on each other and make fun of each other. It was never safe – who was getting picked on – because five minutes later we would turn on someone else.' The digs that flew around including Vaughn mocking Luke's film *Legally Blonde* alongside Reese Witherspoon, calling it *Legally Bland*.

Remarking on the film, and his upturn in fortune, Will said to Den Of Geek: 'I got lucky. I left *Saturday Night Live* without a film to go to, and I'd filmed *Old School* while I was in my last season of the show, and that hadn't come out yet. I was a free agent, in a way, but I knew it was time to leave the show and test the water. The first three movies leaving the show were *Old School*, *Elf* and *Anchorman*, so I had those three in a row that were good ones.'

The BBC said about the film: 'Turning this unlikely set-up into a comedy goldmine, *Road Trip* director Todd Phillips breathes new life into the gross-out formula ... Trading on the combined charms of Wilson, Vaughn, and *Saturday Night Live*'s Will Ferrell, not to mention a killing performance from Jeremy Piven as the university's uptight dean, *Old School* turns out to be something more than just another *Road Trip* American Pie rip-off. It's a hilariously funny and unexpectedly warm look at three men who just want to be boys again. With all the silliness that wish entails.' *Rolling Stone* remarked: 'Only fitfully funny, except when Ferrell is onscreen – then you won't stop laughing', while AskMen.com stated: 'Rotten Tomatoes has *Old School* listed at a barely fresh 60%, but it doesn't take into account the appeal it had for the average moviegoer. Not only was this a huge hit in theatres, but it became a film that people quoted freely and often, some of the lines becoming part of the cultural lexicon (like, "Once it hits your lips, it's so good!"). It's also the film that helped introduce Will Ferrell to the masses and helped Vince Vaughn find his footing as a comedy superstar. The characters that they cultivate in this film (the gentle buffoon and the caddish loudmouth, respectively) helped to shape and define their careers for the next decade. Perhaps *Old School* isn't the most shining example of what film is capable of, but it does what it is supposed to do: It makes you laugh hysterically.'

Old School was a box-office hit, scoring an impressive $75 million at the domestic box office. Lad comedy would soon be a new boom at the box office, and with films that followed like *Starsky & Hutch* and *Wedding Crashers* (both featuring hilarious cameos by Ferrell), as well as *Dodgeball*, the media would soon label the regular roster of comedians that starred in the films – Ferrell,

Luke and Owen Wilson, Vince Vaughn and Ben Stiller – as being members of the Frat Pack.

Ferrell said, however: 'It doesn't really exist, this Frat Pack. We run into each other on occasions and we all like each other's films, I guess, but there isn't some big funny restaurant or bar where we all hang out. At least, if there is, they haven't invited me. I wasn't in *You, Me and Dupree*, Luke Wilson's last movie, and none of them was in *Talladega Nights* with me and, actually, nobody gives a shit.' (*The Observer*, 19.11.2006) Despite his misgivings about the tag when asked years later, it did seem he was more fond of it following their early spate of films, with Will saying at the time: 'Well there's this kind of comedy community that's forming. We all think each other are funny and are all just willing to be in each other's movies. You know we called in some favours and it just works really well. There are some surprises as to who you see and the type of characters that they get to play.' (LOVEFiLM interview, 4.2.2014)

The Frat Pack tag was first labelled in a story in *USA Today* in 2004, and it stuck, a lot less than the first attempt to coin a name for this new Hollywood group that were blazing a trail at the box office. *USA Today* called them the Slacker Pack, no doubt aware that the Frat Pack had been used a few years earlier to describe the rising young talents of Leonardo DiCaprio, Ben Affleck and Matt Damon. However, the term Frat Pack stuck for the crazy comedic group. 'They're almost like a comedy troupe with a new episode every few months,' said

Brandon Gray, a box-office analyst in Los Angeles. 'All of their movies seem to have the same goofy tone to them – they're very light, with a bit of parody, and often devoid of any connective tissue between the scenes.'

The tag would eventually dissipate, with Vaughn adding years later to USA Today: 'I love working with those guys and have had a lot of fun, and I would love to do stuff with them again. But the whole Rat Pack-Frat Pack thing that came out is overblown. It was really Ben Stiller giving opportunities to people. There was never a conscious movement of "Hey, let's all do this."'

CHAPTER EIGHT

FESTIVE FUN

Will had found that role that he had been desperate to land on the big screen, but following up on that success could have been a tricky one. Except on this occasion, Will had a script tailor-made for his abilities. The film would be *Elf*, an old-fashioned festive feel-good romp that was unabashedly filled with big-screen warmth. Ferrell would play an elf who learns that he is human and heads back to New York City to find his family. It's a classic fish-out-of-water story, and one that Will was perfect for.

Said Ferrell to IGN:, 'It was a spec script. I was on a short list of people they had in mind. David [Berenbaum], the writer, said he always had the movie *Big* in mind as something to emulate. He felt like I had some of those Tom Hanks qualities. He always thought I would be well-suited to this role. When Jon Favreau and I first started talking we agreed that if there was any movie we'd want to be compared to, it would be *Big* because that's such a nice film. It's funny but it works on a dramatic level as well.' The script had been warm in Ferrell's hands for a while, but he knew the tone had to be judged perfectly for it to work, reasoning: 'If we could find a way to handle it correctly and shoot, the appeal of it was to be able to shoot a film that would be funny but also heartfelt and be a different type of thing for me to do in terms of something that a family audience would see as opposed to some of the other projects that I have gotten to work on which have obviously been for a different audience. That was the appeal. To have the potential to be in something like this.'

It was handed to Jon Favreau to get the tricky tone just right. The writer and star of *Swingers* was tasked with making a family film that would appeal to grown-up audiences as well. A family man himself, Favreau knew how to make it work. In an interview (Combustible Celluloid, 24.10.2003) he said: 'I have kids now and I'm watching all this stuff, and I can tell the difference. With *Finding Nemo*, you can tell how enthusiastic the filmmakers are. John Lasseter loves the movies he's making. He's not putting crap out for kids to eat up. He's making movies that he wants to see.' However, he added: 'Kids will like whatever. Kids will like Will in an elf suit banging his head. So the kids are going to dig it, but how do you make the parents like it?'

There were two films in particular that he saw as an inspiration – *Being There*, a comedy-drama featuring Peter Sellers, and *Big*, a warm 1998 fantasy-comedy, where a young boy wakes up and finds out he has transformed into an adult body. Both had fish-out-of-water concepts, and Favreau added: 'Those were movies with similar concepts, where it played very real and very emotional. And they were good movies, not just funny movies. This really could have been one long sketch if Will hadn't really treated the character in a way that it changes over the course of the movie.' Jon himself had made more adult fare, and this was all new to him. He told Movies.About.com: 'It's the first movie I made since I've had kids. But it's the first one, certainly, that's appropriate. Even *Daredevil* which sort of skewed young, is still incredibly violent. *Rudy* is appropriate for maybe older kids, but this is probably the first one that they'll ever see that I'm involved with, as they grow up.'

When asked about the character, Ferrell told IGN: 'When I read the script, I thought he had to be the most unjaded creature. There's not a single cynical part of him. I thought it must be played in complete earnest, without any winking to the audience in any way. It had to be played straight. And Jon Favreau shared the same belief. Hopefully, the comedy would come from his unjaded view of things we take for granted.' Producer Jon Berg said: 'Will has such a well-defined sense of himself. He's really gifted physically. And he's incredibly understated:

with just a raised eyebrow or a look he can crack you up. Will is like Peter Sellers: he can make a mundane situation really funny just by the way he manipulates his body.'

Gruff film actor James Caan noted in the film's production notes: 'In this film everybody had to play it straight except for Will. It was like walking through a room of elephants having to make believe everything is normal and that was hard to do. It takes a greater level of concentration, you know, not to see the elephants.' In fact, Will told Collider: 'You just embrace the clash. I mean, I remember doing *Elf* and James Caan like the whole time like I could just tell was looking at me like, what are you doing? In fact, afterwards he said, "I got to hand it to you: I thought you played it way too big the whole time, but it worked out."' And producer Todd Komarnicki added: 'Will is a genius because he combines the silent acting and disciplined comedy of Jacques Tati and Charlie Chaplin with an acrobatic intellect. His ability to explode with vulnerability or implode with happiness makes it impossible to take your eyes off him. You are always waiting to see what he'll do next.'

Like in *Old School*, Ferrell made sure his character had a degree of vulnerability amidst the craziness to ground the movie. Jon stated: 'If you don't have a good story and an emotional aspect to the story people grow weary of just one comic bit after the next. I think they want to see a story that engages them on an emotional level.' Describing the look of his character, Ferrell said: 'It started with the curly hair. I just started to grow it out. It gets that curly. We pretty much hoped that being in an elf suit would be enough. We hoped it would be the kind of thing where you think it's funny when you first see it and then you forget about it and then you start laughing about it again because it keeps adding to the context.' And he added that once again there was only one way to play the part – inhibited : 'That's what I think works the best, and what I think makes the best comedy – something that's completely committed and more approached as an acting exercise, as opposed to being worried about whether to be funny or not. The comedy comes from the context.'

According to *Empire* magazine: 'An uncanny gift for physical comedy helps Will Ferrell propel this festive family movie along, even though it's barely more than a string of sketches held together by a conventional plot. His giant-among-elves character first amuses with his mere size, but in New York he's an outcast of a different kind: a wide-eyed, relentlessly cheerful child in a man's body whose elf-talk convinces everyone he's a nutjob. ... The gags swing between mildly inventive and screamingly obvious, but even the latter are performed and timed well enough to draw a laugh. The plot, however, is so over-shadowed by comic set-pieces that its ending fails to deliver the emotional impact it should. And it doesn't help that the supporting characters are either over-exposed (we see far too much of Buddy's father at his work, for example) or underdeveloped (love interest Jovie is likeable but sidelined).' *Entertainment Weekly* stated:

'Will Ferrell wears lime-green couture and a humiliation-proof grin in a disarmingly funny holiday comedy about an elf-raised foundling who comes to elf-challenged NYC to find his father.' *Time Out*, too, had praise for it: ' Some humour might sail over the heads of the very young, but there's a higher chuckle rate for the grown-ups than much dread "family" fare.'

Not everyone was enamoured of *Elf*, however. Noted film critic Mark Kermode said: 'There are few things scarier than the "creative trajectory" which has led hip gunslinger Jon Favreau from fronting the terrific indie-hit *Swingers* to helming the godawful festive romp *Elf*. Like Schwarzenegger's vomit-inducing *Jingle All the Way* or Tim Allen's repugnant *Santa Clause* series, *Elf* tries its damnedest to hit all the cutesy kids-Crimbo pic buttons while still offering knowing satirical nudges for the poor beleaguered parents. The result is a turkey, despite the presence of Bob Newhart's crotchety narrator and James Caan's cynical children's book publisher, whose group brainstorming sessions produce "a story about a tribe of asparagus children who are self-conscious about the way their pee smells". Yes, I know it looks funny on paper, but after 90 laughter-free minutes you'll be remembering *Scrooged* as the Citizen Kane of Christmas movies, and hankering for the days of *Christmas Slay* and its immortal tagline, "He knows if you've been bad or good – and he's got an axe!"'

Apart from the few Bah Humbug critics, it was still a feel-good film that was a hit for the festive season.

Despite its box-office success and favourable reviews from critics, Will had a nagging doubt about its box-office potential. It's typical of the fearlessness trait he has imbued in himself that he still threw himself into the role while holding fears, recalling: '*Elf* has become this big holiday movie, and I remember running around the streets of New York in tights saying, "This could be the last movie I ever make", and I could never have predicted that it'd become such a popular film.'

He added: 'There was a wide array of reactions. The predominant one of New Yorkers was to walk right by me. If they didn't see a camera close by, people were afraid of me. They made a point of walking around me. I would walk up and hug people and they'd get really upset. A couple of times, they recognised me. People would look at me and say, "Hey, aren't you that guy from *Saturday Night Live*? Have you gone completely insane?" There were some catcalls of "Nice tights".' Indeed, Favreau felt that it was his job as a director to put Ferrell into various awkward situations to see how the funny-man would cope, conceding that the more potentially embarrassing the scenarios were, the funnier Ferrell made them. He said to Movies.About.com, 'Will will usually do more. I never really asked Will to do anything specifically. He would always come up with a really exciting choice. He has very good instincts, especially with physical comedy. My only job when we're doing the broad stuff was to either build him sets that he could play off of, put him in a costume that he could really work, or suggest things that might inspire him to try something different and go further than he had. But he's a performer and so if that camera was rolling, he would use that as an opportunity to go for it.'

Favreau told Movies.About.com: 'We come from a similar background. Will studied at the Groundlings. I studied at Second City. He came through *Saturday Night Live* and certainly I was influenced a great deal by the people who were on that show. A lot of people I worked with have worked on that show. We both have very similar sensibilities and a similar way of working, coming from an improv background. Although he didn't improvise dialogue that much, I was not afraid to put him in situations that were unplanned. And as a matter of fact, the last day of shooting in New York, we just took cameras. We didn't even have the director of photography. We just took a cameraman and a film loader and some PAs and went around the city in a van, jumped out and threw people some money and got to use all different locations, like him getting his shoe shined or him crossing the street, with all real people around him. I put him in those situations and he had to improvise and stay in character while dealing with people who, for the most part, didn't even know they were in a movie.'

Elf is now a regular for festive TV, something Jon had hoped for when making the film, saying: 'I get excited being in an audience. I'll know I did my job on this movie if it pops up on TV every year. That'll be the real test of time. I got spoiled because *Rudy* did. That pops up every year around Thanksgiving, and *Swingers* is on cable all the time now. Those are two movies that didn't make the most [money] of any movies I've ever made, and [weren't] necessarily the best reviewed. But they were the ones that made a ripple in our culture and have stood the test of time.'

He added to Movies.About.com, 'In making *Elf*, on the one hand, you could make a movie about Christmas that's just utter crap and parents will take the kids to go see it and there's a very low bar. But the upside is if you make something that really has emotional resonance and that you put a lot of care into, it could become part of our culture for years to come, and be played like no other movie is ever played. *It's a Wonderful Life* was really a nothing movie when it came out, but it has emerged as something that's very important to our society and our culture. And still, if I turn it on and there's 10 minutes left in it, I'll keep it on, and sit down and watch it. I'll be in tears. It's embarrassing. You're getting ready to go out, putting your tie on, your wife finds you sitting at the foot of the bed watching the TV and you're all teared up. That's something that's like the brass ring for a Christmas movie. We always set out to make something that we knew, if we did our job right, that this could turn into something that people would see year after year.'

The film was such a hit that a sequel was a no-brainer. However, Will was reluctant to make a follow-up movie, reasoning that the film worked well on its own. And after it was reported that he turned down nearly $30 million to reprise the role, he was asked if he ever regretted turning down that kind of money. He joked to the A.V. Club: 'I do. Whenever I'm at the boat show. You know, when I'm looking at these 08 yachts that are for sale, I think "I could have just walked in with a briefcase of cash and put it on the table and walked out with a yacht."'

He did answer the question seriously, however, claiming: 'No. Well, not when the concept of the sequel didn't feel like it worked at all. In fact, that's the only way I could have made that movie. Because I kept telling the studio, and obviously for them, it's a total opportunity, you know, "Let's make a sequel, da-da-da!" I don't know what the sequel is. It's like a fish-out-of-water story, and he's now in the water. Where do you go? I go "Prove me wrong." The script was kind of written, and I was like, "This makes no sense." And I thought, the only way I could do this movie is to blatantly say, if I was promoting it, "I did it for the money. The movie is completely flawed, it doesn't make sense as a premise. So yes, I did it for $29 million." Because otherwise, it would have been, "Buddy the Elf doesn't fight for the kid, he's kind of indoctrinated, but not really, and he's still fascinated by an ATM!" It just didn't work, so it was a very easy decision.'

He was also asked to star in a sequel to *Old School*, but turned it down, saying: 'Oh, I wouldn't do another *Old School*. They put these rumours out there, these studio people, but I would never be behind that one.'

For his next film, Will went off on a different tack –

starring in Woody Allen's *Melinda and Melinda*. Allen is no stranger to assembling an all-star cast, with Jonny Lee Miller, Chiwetel Ejiofor, Amanda Peet and Chloe Sevigny all joining Ferrell for the New-York-based film, which focuses on two viewpoints of the same situation – one comedic, one dramatic. Said Allen in the film's production notes: 'It's something that occurs to me many times in my movies. They can often be treated comically or dramatically, and I usually opt to treat them comically. But it occurred to me that you could get a story and you could fool around with it both ways. For me, it's just chance. This was just the idea that came out of the box. I have a lot of ideas for stories. They come to me all the time.'

The famed comic writer is known for being precious with the words on his scripts and lots of actors don't ever get to see the full script. Actress Radha Mitchell was one of the lucky few that got a script. She told About.com Hollywood Movies: 'I did. I'm glad that I did, too, because there's a lot of dialogue. I mean, it's dialogue-driven. I remember one day he said, "Can you come in and do that monologue?" And it's like a two-page monologue and it wasn't on the schedule. [Laughing] I'm like, "OK …" I was glad that I had had access to the script and that I'd been reading it, and it had become a part of my life before coming to set. … We didn't rehearse. We weren't really even supposed to meet each other. Chiwetel [Ejiofor], one of the actors in the movie, had come in from London so he called everybody –

everyone that was around and we all had brunch. It was sort of this never-ending brunch we had with Will Ferrell that went from like 11:00 [am] to 1:00 in the morning. It went from uptown right to downtown. So we did get to know each other at first. But if it was the way Woody planned, we wouldn't have at all. We would have just come to set and said the lines.'

When asked about her experiences working with Woody and Will, she said: 'At times they would sort of anecdote each other so you wouldn't get a sense of either of them. But at other times they'd both be on, and it'd be hilarious.' Talking about the experience, Will noted (Shakefire.com): 'He's one of the few people. He was like you can say these words or not, this is the script but if you don't feel like … and so this one time I was like OK great, thank you so much. Then I left out a joke and everything. He was like, "you left out the thing, the joke" and I was like "well yeah you said like if I don't." "I know but I think this is really funny." So I was like OK, I get it. Say what he wrote.' Mitchell added (About.com Hollwood Movies): 'Woody would come up to us and say, "Just say it however you want. Do whatever you want." Then he'd come up to us and say, "Is that how you're going to do it?" That would make sure that we'd both stick to the script. You don't really want to change [the words]. It's a genius who's written them. So there's something about them that you want to keep.' Ejiofor told Cinemareview.com: 'I thought it was strange to work that way, but I enjoyed it. You're wholly focused on your character and your storyline.'

The script took a month to write, with only his most trusted collaborators seeing the piece, including longtime casting director Juliet Taylor, co-producer Helen Robin, production designer Santo Loquasto and producer Aronson. Producer Aronson said in the film's production notes: 'I thought it was a brilliant idea conceptually. From one person's perspective a story can be funny; from another person's perspective it can be sad. Woody is brilliant at recognising those aspects of the way people think and operate. You and I may see it, but we don't isolate it like he does. He's very perceptive, and he brings that to bear on a situation.' Will was one of the few actors who were given the full script, and he noted: 'I loved the structure of the whole movie – these two parallel stories which were illustrating the point of the fine line between comedy and tragedy. It was so imaginative and unique but at the same time very signature Woody Allen.'

When asked about the casting of Will, Woody said: 'You can cast a comic actor in a serious role and they do a good job. The other way around doesn't work very well. My movies tend to be more sophisticated than the films Will is known for. But he did a great job.' Producer Aronson said: 'When we got Will Ferrell, he really hadn't been in anything, just *Saturday Night Live*. He proved himself to be a very versatile actor. He has the ability to be a real, sophisticated, romantic comedy lead.' Will said about the character: 'He's obviously a comedic character, but it was the most realistic type of character that I've gotten to play. He's a real person as opposed to an arch[etype]. It was nice because you could rely on basic dialogue between people, not funny costumes, and there wasn't so much pressure to be funny. The humour is already there in the context of the story.' (Cinemareview.com)

The film opened slowly in the US, debuting on one screen in New York, but it proved to be successful with audiences, and despite the limited release in the US, it grossed over $3 million domestically, and it took a further $17 million worldwide, reflecting the appeal of Woody's films for European audiences.

Reviews for the movie were mixed. CNN stated: 'As is the case with many longtime Woody Allen fans, I approach his annual film with a combination of high hopes and a heavy heart. His movies in recent years – to put it mildly – have been wildly uneven. His latest effort, *Melinda and Melinda* is his best in a while, but still pales next to his brilliant films of the 1970s and part of the 90s.' The review also praised Will for his performance as a Woody surrogate – a term for Woody Allen's later movies, in which he cast other actors in parts that would have been played by him in the past. 'Past Allen surrogates have included John Cusack (*Bullets Over Broadway*) and Jason Biggs (*Anything Else*), both of whom more or less tried to channel Allen with varying degrees of success. However, Ferrell makes the character completely his own and provides the film with its most hilarious moments. The range of expressions crossing his face in a scene where he finds his wife in bed with another man is worth the price of admission.'

Empire magazine gave the film four out of five stars, adding: 'The film begins with the most explicit amplification of the dynamic that has consumed Allen's creativity – the pull between tragedy and comedy. *Melinda and Melinda* tackles these seemingly polar opposites head on, combining the straight-up laughs of "The Early, Funny Stuff" with the gravitas of "The Later, Serious Works", creating Allen's funniest, most affecting movie for some time. Part of the thrill here is that, in many ways, *Melinda and Melinda* is a melting pot of Allen's best work, touching base in particular with *Manhattan*, *Broadway Danny Rose* and *Hannah and Her Sisters*. But if M&M negotiates typical Woody territory – the vagaries of romance, breakdowns in communication ("Of course we communicate, but can we not talk about it?"), identity and intimacy – it does it with a sharpness that's been absent in the *Deconstructing Harry/Anything Else* era.'

New York Magazine was less impressed with the movie, adding: 'The press kit that accompanies *Melinda* is larded with the usual gush from the cast about what an honour it is to be chosen by Allen ("I was so awed by the fact that Woody would even ask me"; "First I had to get over the headline of 'Being in a Woody Allen Movie'"). It's both touching and baffling. Yes, Allen has given us *Annie Hall*, *Hannah and Her Sisters*, a delightful trifle like *Manhattan Murder Mystery*, and the gratifyingly tough-minded *Deconstructing Harry*, which tapped into the bracing vulgarity of his early comedies. But when are we going to get a generation of actors who will finally decline to succumb to The Woody Mystique, and refuse to accept a proffered role without first deciding whether the entire damn project is worthwhile?'

It was Will's first real attempt at tackling something different to his over-the-top comedic performances, but it wouldn't be the last. However, he would star in another film that would change everything. It was time to put on the moustache, get into the impeccably tailored suit and step away from the mahogany bookcase. It was a time to Stay Classy.

CHAPTER NINE

I'M KIND OF A BIG DEAL

This writer's first viewing of *Anchorman* was in a cramped press-screening room, usually the location for the films that aren't blockbusters. Indeed, the screening room was only half full, but still early hopes were high given the film's wacky trailer. Within a few minutes it was clear that this was a special but divisive film. A lot of the critics in the London screening room were audibly unimpressed, with the rest guffawing loudly. In fact, when the song 'Afternoon Delight' is sung in the office, some critics left, completely unsure of what they were watching. Their exit was barely noticed as the ones who were 'getting it' were in fits of laughter.

Will Ferrell plays Ron Burgundy, a chauvinistic local anchorman of the 1970s. It would be Ferrell at his greatest, a bumbling buffoon of a man imbued with a touch of vulnerability, as his cocksure approach subtly masks his insecurity. *Anchorman* was that rare breed from a *SNL* performer. While Ron Burgundy wasn't a character that starred in the studios of 30 Rock, it could have been argued that there have been several prototypes of Burgundy, notably Will's version of veteran crooner Rob Goulet. Thus the film retained the very best spirit of *SNL*. It was pure madcap madness, filled with the inescapable feeling that anything could happen. Sustaining that for a movie is a rare gift however, and there are few that can lay claim to such a success. The *Wayne's World* movies could, as could *SNL*-cast-heavy *Caddyshack* or the early Steve Martin films like *The Man With Two Brains* or *The Jerk*. It's a film packed with highlights, with people picking several different moments as their favourite – a sign of a great comedy. It features hugely quotable dialogue and scenes that just get better with repeated viewings, a film that practically begs more watches – another sign of a great comedy.

While it's Ferrell's film, he is more than comfortable to be surrounded by other great comedy actors – all bringing a different set of comedic skills. There is Paul Rudd's male bravado tinged with insecurity, Tank with his over-the-top machismo, Steve Carell's mastery of deadpan, the always dependable Fred Willard as the head of the news and Christina Applegate – the actress who not only plays the straight 'man' role with assured calmness but is also willing to get her hands dirty when it comes to the physical comedy. Throw in delightful cameos from Vince

Vaughn, Ben Stiller, Tim Robbins, Luke Wilson and you've got a film that just constantly surprises. It was a hit – if a slow-burning one. But due to word of mouth its popularity rose.

The film would be a huge launching pad for the actors involved. Carell's performance as Brick would kick-start a hugely successful leading-man career – a path that was trodden similarly by Paul Rudd. Rudd had first found fame as the charismatically gentle stepbrother of Alicia Silverstone's character in *Clueless*, and had followed it up with several romantic leading-man roles with diminishing results at the box office. However, his comedic turn as Brian Fantana saw him star in other comedies, such as *Role Models*, *Knocked Up* and *Man, I Love You*.

Anchorman was directed by Adam McKay – someone who worked with Will on *SNL*. McKay was on writing duties for *SNL* but showed his directorial ambition by bringing back *SNL*'s digital short films. Adam said: 'I was going to quit the show. I had been head writer for a couple of years and there was all this stuff I wanted to try, but ultimately it's his [Lorne Michaels'] show and I should politely move on. My manager said, "If you're going to quit, make an unreasonable demand. What would you want in your dream world?" I didn't want to go to production meetings. I didn't want to be in the room for the actual show any more, which is actually no fun. I wanted a raise. I wanted a budget for short films. And I wanted to name my own screen credit. Lorne said yes. So for the last two years I was there, I was coordinator of falconry. That was my actual screen credit. Wow, some people were [ticked off]! I'm like, "Relax, this is a comedy show."' (*Chicago Tribune*, 28.4.2012)

One of the shorts that he filmed was *The H Is O*, aka *The Heat is On*, a memorable sketch show which featured Ferrell and Stiller in a bizarre sexual encounter. Said McKay: 'To this day, I bump into people who whisper, "Hey, the H is O." It's like a secret club. And that was also kind of intentional. I never strove to make those shorts popular. It was more like I was going to film school. I had a crew. I had a budget. I shot 16 mm. I was shooting digital by the second year of this. I made a dozen films all together. I wouldn't have known how to direct *Anchorman* if I hadn't shot those videos. But also, some of them were just too crazy for the format. They were not as populist as what the guys at Lonely Island (Andy Samberg and Co.) are doing on the show now. Those guys grew up making shorts, like a lot of people we hire at Funny or Die. Digital is fluid to them – it's a second language.' (*Chicago Tribune*, 28.4.2012)

The idea for *Anchorman* came from a serious documentary that Will watched which charted the rise of women in the TV newsroom, and how they managed to break into the male-dominated news areas of the 1970s. He told the website LoveFilm: 'I was watching a documentary on news programmes in the 70s, and at the point that I was watching it, this gentleman comes on talking about working with women for the first time in the 70s. He was very blunt about the fact that, although he had come a long way now, at the time, he wasn't very nice to her at all. He kept on saying "You have to remember, back then I was a real male chauvinist pig – I hated women." That statement just seemed so funny to me and it just went from there. The film is a comedy first, but as we pieced it together we started to realise that it's still the same now, it hasn't really changed that much. TV networks learnt early on about the possibilities of marketing and advertising as they realised that people were less reliant on papers and were using the TV news as their only source of information. So it's interesting and scary really, whichever way you want to look at it, that this is a lot of people's only source of information.'

Will added: 'I called Adam with an idea to do a script about the petulant male-dominated world of the newsroom and how these men dealt with a woman for the first time, and he said "Great, let's do it."' And in an interview with *Index Magazine*, Will said: 'When I was a kid, I loved watching the news on TV. The news teams fascinated me because I thought they all hung out together. It certainly sounded that way from the stupid banter between stories – "Boy, Pete, that looks like your golf swing. Ha ha ha." So I wanted to write a story about a male newscaster in the 70s, when the feminist movement was emerging, who has to work with a female newscaster for the first time. He's a big fish in a little pond, and he's really close to his news team. I was asking myself, what kind of petulant behaviour would result?' After watching the documentary, McKay recalled: 'There were all these interviews with anchormen of the day who were talking about how upset they had been that a woman had come in to work with them. We were laughing so hard at these guys with perfect ties admitting that they were completely freaked out by a woman coming into the news office.'

The pair would spend their days cramped in a hotel, with index cards, detailing their ideas, plastered over the walls. Will said to Index Magazine: 'When we wrote the script, we holed up in a room at the Wyndham Village Hotel for week-long stretches. We started by brain-storming, just thinking of ideas – small ideas or big ones – for stories and scenes. We'd sit with a pen and paper and write them all down.' They wanted to make a comedy that was incredibly broad, but still had enough depth that you cared about the characters. In an interview in *Index Magazine*, they cited the early classic episodes of *The Simpsons* as an inspiration:

WILL: A lot of people who read the script said, 'It's funny, but it's weird.'

ADAM: The movie has more in common with *The Simpsons* than with your standard Hollywood comedy. The writers on that show combine really stupid and really smart comedy. That was our goal – we wanted to be smart-dumb.

WILL: *Anchorman* has the broadest jokes in the world.

ADAM: It does have boner jokes. It also has

references to Tennyson and existentialism. Ron Burgundy plays jazz flute. It's kind of all over the place.

WILL: We were going to make Ron Burgundy a big, broad, balls-to-the-wall kind of character, but we discovered that it was funnier to see him get emotional – to see him talking in a whisper. You can't have a character on the ceiling all the time.

ADAM: We were looking for Burgundy's emotional range. We thought it was important to let him be sensitive and get distraught.

WILL: The audience is laughing at him, but they also experience that pang – 'I hate to say it, but I feel sorry for the guy.'

Famed comedy director and writer Judd Apatow came on board as producer, with executive producer Shauna Robertson also helping to develop the screenplay. Judd was delighted to work on the film, as he had been a fan of McKay in the past, telling the film's production notes: 'Adam punched up a script that I was trying to develop. I thought he was truly one of the funniest guys I had ever come across. [And] I have been a fan of Will's for years. I think he is hilarious and had always hoped that I would have the opportunity to work with him. Together, Will and Adam are two of the nicest guys that you could collaborate with. They are extremely talented and have a great time working together, and that becomes infectious and raises the level of everyone's work.' Robertson joked:

'I wouldn't be surprised if Adam and Will were twins separated at birth. They have the exact same sense of humour. It's really random to find two people who work together so well.'

The film gets the 1970s period look perfectly. Discussing how he came up with the look of Ron, Will told LoveFilm: 'He just kept on evolving, I knew he wanted a moustache and in terms of hair, well, we didn't think my hair was good enough. We wanted it to be this big pouf of hair, held in place by loads of hairspray, so in the end we had to settle with a wig to achieve that one.' Costume designer Debra McGuire added in the film's production notes: 'I loved the idea that his name was Ron Burgundy and decided that the colour burgundy would be a good place to start in his costumes.' And talking about his character, Will revealed to Visimag.com in 2004: 'It was such a fun era to look back on. We've kind of forgotten now what it was like because, for the most part, things have become more equal in terms of gender roles. But when you look back at the attitudes then, it seems so silly. It's great to be able to play on the fact that these guys are male chauvinists. We are not glorifying male chauvinists, we are making fun of them. Ron thinks he is a lot smarter and more talented than he really is. He has somehow gotten by on his charisma and although he is – let's face it – a terrible journalist, San Diego just loves him.'

The film charts the lives of the newsroom men and the moment that everything changes – the introduction of Veronica Corningstone, a woman who will break the male-dominated stranglehold in the newsroom. It would be a tricky character to play: a straight woman who could handle the jokes that flew past her – many improvised – but could also make sure she had such a presence that audiences would care for her. Christina Applegate was cast in the role – a veteran of comedy, with her famous role as the pretty daughter in *Married With Children*, a hugely popular sitcom in the 1980s and 1990s. McKay said about her casting: 'We had to get the perfect person. Without exaggerating, I think we read more than 100 actresses for that role, but no one fit the bill. Then Christina walked in, and that was it. She's such a good actress and so funny, and she can improvise, which is important when you're working with Will, so we just had to have her.' Applegate added: 'When I got the script, I thought it was really hysterical, and I could see Will Ferrell as Ron Burgundy. The whole idea really appealed to me. If you look back at tapes of newscasters during the early 70s, they seem incredibly misogynistic. No offence to any of them, but it was a man's world. You could smoke and even have your scotch while doing the newscast; it was just a completely different world run by these very macho men. So, that's what Veronica steps into. They have their perfect world where they have everything under control, and in walks Veronica and turns everything upside down.' (Cinemareview.com)

It was a perfect comedy, but not everybody expected it to be a hit, with Will admitting: 'Of all the stuff Adam McKay has done, we've always said "I don't know if anyone else will like it, but I think that's funny." The studio didn't understand it. The head of marketing was openly telling the media, "I don't get it." We didn't care, because we got to make exactly what we wanted to make, and we were happy, even if it was the last movie we ever made.' (Den of Geek, 2.12.2010) While it may have been a struggle to market the film, there was such an appeal in Frat Pack films that the audiences would have come purely for the cast – the fact that it was a surreal, bonkers and way-out-of-there movie was just an added bonus.

The reviews were initially a mixed bag. *Time Out* said: 'As *Starsky & Hutch* proved, 70s men are an easy comic target. They can be reduced to familiar stereotypes, while providing a source of guilt-free sexist gags. Such gags result when *Anchorman* Ron Burgundy Will Ferrell and pals get their flares in a flap about ambitious new employee Veronica Corningstone (Christina Applegate). No sooner has Ron wooed her than she's stepping into his shoes. Will he accept her success graciously? No, he'll bellow obscure insults from the rooftops and pound his hairy chest at the shame of being eclipsed by a female. In this world, being an anchorman is the ultimate masculine prize. As Veronica's power increases, her male colleagues weaken. Their pride can only be reclaimed by rescuing Veronica from bears in a zoo ("We bears are a proud race. They must pay for their intrusion," the creatures growl via subtitles, before grudgingly accepting newcomers as the anchormen do).' The review added: 'But plot isn't the primary interest here: this is as flimsy as a sitcom, and it's shot like one too. Like a *Saturday Night Live* sketch, it's propelled by its absurd humour, from silly erection jokes to hilariously surreal exchanges ("What? ... You know I don't speak Spanish," Ron admonishes his barking dog). This takes a joke and runs with it – sometimes too far, but usually long enough to wear you down and force you to submit to its craziness. With cameos from chums Ben Stiller, Jack Black, Luke Wilson and Vince Vaughn, the film smacks of self-indulgence, but throws enough comic talent at the screen to make it stick. This particular boys' club isn't facing extinction just yet.'

The *Washington Post* added: 'It's a skit, but so ingeniously constructed and convincingly executed that it manages to sustain its energy far beyond sketch length. It never becomes tedious and strained ... It's certainly the role that Ferrell was born to play: It caters exactly to his strengths – the hyper-exaggerated mannerisms of the *Saturday Night Live* sketch – and avoids his weaknesses, which would be something called "replicating believable human behaviour".' Peter Travers from *Rolling Stone* said, '*Anchorman* slaps a goofy smile on your face', while Ebert noted: 'If the movie simply focused on making Ron and his team look ridiculous, it might grow tedious, because that would be such an easy thing to do. But it has a kind of sweetness to it. Despite his weaknesses, Ron is sort of a nice guy, darn it all, and Veronica Corningstone, despite her desire to project a serious image, kinda likes the guy – especially when he reveals an unsuspected musical talent in a lounge one night, after he's asked to "sit in on jazz flute".'

The *New York Post* wasn't as keen, saying: 'Ferrell is funny spouting his weird stream-of-consciousness rants, but too often the plot leaves him hanging and he resorts to just Yelling Really Loud.' The *San Francisco Chronicle* stated: 'Though always sophomoric and sometimes bland, *Anchorman* is also intermittently funny, with just enough laughs (but only just enough) to keep an audience rooting for it. The movie's strenuous pursuit of comic moments, in fact, becomes a comic strategy in itself. There's a scene in which Will Ferrell, as the vain and empty-headed Ron Burgundy, is mourning the loss of his pet dog. He calls a co-worker from a pay phone, sobbing and shrieking, and it's supposed to be funny, but it's not really. But Ferrell keeps it going, sobbing louder, shrieking louder, flailing in the phone booth, taking the moment past exaggeration and past absurdity into some comedy version of outer space. He gets his laugh. Ferrell has to work this hard because *Anchorman* is a satire without much truth or perception behind it and therefore no satiric kick.'

Costing over $25 million, the film got its money back in its opening weekend, and went on to gross nearly $100 million in the US alone. And the film would grow even more, with repeated viewings sparking even more quotable dialogue and the film a regular inclusion in best-of-comedy film lists. At the end of 2004, the film has already built such a loyal following that McKay put together a follow-up DVD entitled *Wake Up, Ron Burgundy*, which comprised cobbled-together excised subplots and deleted scenes from the first movie. In the UK, *Wake Up, Ron Burgundy* was released as a newly-packaged DVD companion piece with the first film.

The slow-burning success surprised its stars. Applegate said: 'When *Anchorman* first opened, I think everyone kind of went, like, "Oh, that's a bummer." But all of a sudden it just started to pick up steam. I remember watching from afar, going "wow".' Suddenly the actors would be greeted by flippant lines they delivered in the midst of hours of improv and messing around on set from crowds of people on the street. Suddenly *Anchorman* had become one of the most quoted movies of all time. Will said: 'Someone sent me and Adam a photo of a troop transport carrier in Baghdad, in the days when the Iraq war was still pretty nasty. Ron Burgundy's face was stencilled on the side and it said "Stay classy, Baghdad". That was one of the craziest.'

Ferrell was becoming a regular on the big screen now, and he thrilled audiences by appearing as a cameo in Todd Phillips' *Starsky & Hutch* – with Den of Geek stating: 'I didn't watch *Starsky & Hutch* episodes when I was a kid, so I can't comment on how the movie compares to the TV series. I can safely say, though, this movie is more parody that a straight adaptation of the show. You'll see occasional tips of the hat to the show like recreations of scenes from the series opening or cameos by the original Starsky & Hutch, Paul Michael Glaser and David Soul. But beyond that there's not much similarity.'

With roles like *Anchorman* and memorable cameo

appearances in *Starsky & Hutch* it was clear that Ferrell was a fully-fledged movie star. Talking about meeting his fans, he told *Rolling Stone*: 'Meeting fans, I'll be like, "Oh, hey, how are you?" And, literally, they're like, "What are you going to do? Do something! Are you sure that's him? He's not doing anything!" Yes, I fear they're horribly underwhelmed.'

But, befitting his new status, he was a regular on the big screen, appearing in six films in 2005. Will Ferrell had arrived.

CHAPTER TEN

WILLING IT BIG AT THE BOX OFFICE

So 2005 was a big year for Will Ferrell, with the comedian an ever-present figure at the box office.

He made an appearance in *The Producers*, a musical based on the 2001 Broadway musical, which was in turn based on the classic 1968 Gene Wilder film comedy. The 2001 Broadway Tony Award-winning musical featured Nathan Lane and Matthew Broderick, and they reprised their award-winning roles on the big screen. Lane stars as a down-and-out-of-luck producer who teams up with Broderick's accountant to put on a surefire stage flop in a bid to scam his investors out of money. However, the play inexplicably becomes a hit.

Nathan Lane said about the musical in the production notes: 'It's always great when people show up to see your work, you know, and I'm always happy about that.

Everything comes in cycles in show-business. There are times when at first they fall in love with you, then they get sick of you and then … then they love you again. It's sort of a natural evolution in show-business. *The Producers* is sort of a once-in-a-lifetime kind of phenomenon and I was very grateful to be a part of it. In terms of the theatre at any rate, I've been doing this for 30 years so it's an audience that has watched me grow up on the stage really. It's sort of the one place where I know that, you know, that people will buy tickets. It's an important thing to be able to fill a theatre because it gives you some choices in terms of your career.'

And, talking about the film, he added: 'Well, Mel [Brooks] first mentioned it while we were recording the cast *album* – nobody will say that any more. I joked with him and said, "Well, you know, Danny DeVito and Ben Stiller will be great in the parts." Really, thanks to the success of *Chicago* it did finally happen. It's unusual for the person who originated the part onstage to do it on film and so I was very grateful and thrilled to be able to do that, because it's a great part and great parts are hard to come by.' He continued: 'The major difference is that there's no audience. You have to let go of that. And because it's a very audience-driven show it's just going back to basics, as you would with any movie. I mean, obviously there's a familiarity with the material and a comfortable feeling of you know this character very well. But it's the same sorts of problems and obstacles. And also you just wanted to give Susan [Stroman, the

Ladies' Man: legendary anchorman Ron Burgundy gets up close and personal with Miley Cyrus at the 2013 MTV Europe Music Awards.
(© *Press Association*)

Above: Sport Fan: Will has appeared in several sports comedies; in fact, he nearly turned his back on the big screen to become a sports broadcaster while he was at university. (© *Press Association*)

Below: The New Class: *Old School*, released in 2003, propelled Will to global fame and saw the arrival of the so-called Frat Pack. (© *Press Association*)

Above left: Family fun: Will and son Magnus Ferrell enjoy some basketball bonding. (© *Press Association*)

Above right: Happily married: Will met his future wife, Viveca Paulin, when she was working at an auction house. They are now one of Hollywood's strongest couples. (© *Press Association*)

Below: Animated personality: Will Ferrell has shown off his vocal talents in a number of animated and CGI family films, including *Curious George* from 2006. (© *Press Association*)

Right: Money man: Will Ferrell's films have earned hundreds of millions at the box office. He is seen here at the Los Angeles premiere of the TV miniseries *Spoils of Babylon* in January 2014.

(*© Press Association*)

Left: In the fast lane: Will and John C. Reilly pose in their *Talladega Nights* costumes at the 2006 MTV Movie Awards.

(*© Press Association*)

Above: Comedy with a cause: Will teams up with music superstar Sting at the Rainforest Foundation Fund Benefit in New York's Carnegie Hall, May 2006.

(© *Press Association*)

Below: Skating on thin ice: Will shows off his ice-skating moves with NBC *Today* host Meredith Vieira while promoting his 2007 comedy hit *Blades of Glory*.

(© *Press Association*)

Left: The primetime pair: Will Ferrell and his *Anchorman* co-star Christina Applegate are all smiles on the red carpet.

(© *Press Association*)

Right: Double Trouble: Will Ferrell and Zach Galifianakis caused comedy mayhem in the 2012 political comedy *The Campaign*.

(© *Press Association*)

Above: Making the news: Ferrell poses happily with his *Anchorman 2* castmates – Paul Rudd, Steve Carell, Christina Applegate and David Koechner – at the London premiere in December 2013. (© *Press Association*)

Below: Staying in character: Will's fictitious TV anchorman is honoured at a news conference at Boston's Emerson College on 5 December 2013.

(© *Press Association*)

Plastic co-star: Will poses with his fellow *Lego Movie* cast mate at the LA premiere of the hugely successful family blockbuster in February 2014.

director], some choices, you know? The material demands a kind of size and theatricality and you have to honour that.'

Broderick told AboutMovies.com: '*The Producers*, just from the minute we started doing it, the audience was like, "Yeah, more. That's what we want." Just the second we started in *Chicago*, audiences loved it. They loved even jokes that weren't very good. They were like, "Fine, that doesn't matter. It's OK." It was longer in *Chicago* and we shortened it. But even when it was too long, they were like, "I don't care." They didn't care. And then it was just one of *those* jobs. I got the job and so did Nathan because we weren't quite as washed up as you might think before *The Producers*. I was working pretty steadily right up to *The Producers*.'

It was always such a pressured role for Broderick as he had to follow in the footsteps of Gene Wilder's iconic performance in the original film. He explained: 'I was always worried about that because I love Gene Wilder so much. I like him in everything, but I can't get his performance [in *The Producers*] out of my head. There's no way. I remember when we started I told Susan Stroman, I was like, "I don't even know how to do this because I can close my eyes and basically watch the whole movie." She said, "Well once you do it over and over again, it'll just drift toward you, hopefully." And that's kind of hopefully what did happen. It just piece by piece … you get your own ideas. Basically I started just with his stuff and a lot of it is really just lifted right from him. But

I think that's like the script, I didn't write the script either, so I'm basing it on words somebody wrote. A lot of the performance is based on him, too, and I hope that is OK. But then I just over time started to get more of my own ideas, and get more of myself into the part, and hopefully that stayed when we went into the movie.'

When asked about the difference about the stage version and the new version, he said: 'That's really what's most fun about a play, is you really have a feeling of living the whole guy, every night. And that's great fun. There's nobody editing. It's just you communicating with the audience and the other actors. It's a great feeling of achievement at the end. Whereas a film, most days you say, "Oh God, I hope I got something, I hope one of those takes was good. This is depressing and there's so much traffic and I'm in the car again. What time is tomorrow? Can't I come a little later, please?" You never get the big, "Well let's go to Joe Allen's and have a martini and celebrate." You don't get that much in films.'

Will played Liebkind, the man whose play, *Springtime for Hitler*, becomes the focal point of the movie.

Time Magazine said: 'A good time is had by all, and the spirit is infectious', while the *Washington Post* said: 'So how good is the movie of the musical of the movie? The answer is: It's pretty good.' However, *Time Out* said: 'Now we get the film of the show of the film, except it's not really much of a movie, more like a recording of the stage version. Theatre director Susan Stroman clearly has little idea how to shape comedy and music for the screen, so she just plonks the camera down and lets the show roll on, allowing the Broadway cast of flamboyant impresario Nathan Lane and ambitious bean-counter Matthew Broderick to play it to the back of the gallery. On celluloid this proves brashly overstated yet somehow lifeless, while the energetic efforts of Will Ferrell's Nazi-loving writer, and a howlingly miscast Uma Thurman as sexy Swedish secretary Ulla, also struggle to raise the spirits.' With a reported budget of $45 million, the film only took less than half of it at the US box office.

Next up for Will was heading back to his Frat Pack pals. He made a memorable cameo appearance in *The Wedding Crashers* – a 2005 comedy featuring his *Old School* pal Vince Vaughn and his *Zoolander* co-star Owen Wilson. The film stars Wilson and Vaughn as two men who crash wedding parties to party, eat free food, drink free and meet lots of women. Their lives take a different turn when they crash the wedding of the daughter of the US Secretary of the Treasury. They end up causing such a splash that they are asked to spend some time with the family – and cue the partying pair falling in love with the other daughters of US state figures.

One of the film's funnier moments sees the appearance of Chazz Reinhold, the man who taught the pair every-thing they need to know about crashing weddings. However, he has now moved on to crashing funerals, believing that women who grieve are desperate for male comfort. Will plays Chazz in an uncredited role, and it's with such a strong impact that he pretty much walks away with the movie, despite his limited screen time.

The movie was a hit with the critics, although many conceded that the comedy did have its faults. *Film4* said: 'The Frat Pack goes from strength to strength in a robust romp that's only marred by the director's apparent inability to say "Cut".' *Empire* gave the movie three out of five stars, saying: 'This summertime rom-com is a mouthwatering prospect indeed: the Frat Pack's hippest stars – Owen Wilson and Vince Vaughn – teamed up as fast-talking rogues; an always-welcome comedy turn from Christopher Walken; and a flamboyant cameo from the daddy of Frat himself, Will Ferrell. To quote Vaughn from *Dodgeball*: "I'm laughing already." As it is, *Wedding Crashers* doesn't quite live up to its promise, but through no fault of its off-the-wall cast. Sharing an easy chemistry and free of the usual joker/straight-guy dynamic, Wilson and Vaughn quip, riff and banter to hilarious effect. And both get their fair share of money moments – the latter's muggings are particularly hysterical in a raunchy dinner-party sequence. That the lead characters' cocksure confidence extends to the movie itself is its biggest weakness. While Vaughn and Wilson are adept at loose-limbed improvisation, that doesn't disguise the fact that the material they're funking up is pretty lazy. Sure, all Chris Walken has to do to score a laugh is narrow his reptilian eyes, but that's no reason not to give the man decent lines. In fact, the only supporting character who doesn't feel watered-down is Isla Fisher's nutso nympho – an unexpected, scene-stealing joy. There's enough good-natured energy to compensate, but the wait for this year's *Dodgeball* continues.'

The film was a huge hit at the box office, with analysts noting that the Frat Pack films were becoming a huge attraction to audiences.

It was a change of pace for Will next. He starred in *Winter Passing*, a low-budget drama, alongside Ed Harris and *Elf* co-star Zooey Deschanel. It was a modest film with modest ambitions. Ebert said: '*Winter Passing* is the story of how Reese (Zooey Deschanel) takes the bus to the Upper Peninsula of Michigan and finds her father, Don Holden (Ed Harris), living not in the family home but in the shack in the backyard. When she knocks on the front door of the big house, it is opened by Corbit (Will Ferrell). Reese says she wants to see her father. Corbit says he wants to see some ID. Later in the movie he confides, "I know karate. I've amassed several belts." This is the kind of movie routinely dismissed as too slow and quiet by those who don't know it is more exciting to listen than to hear. It is sure to disappoint those attracted by the promise of a Will Ferrell comedy – disappoint, puzzle, maybe enrage. What you hope for are those Ferrell fans who are open to a new kind of film they may not have seen before. That's how you grow as a filmgoer; your favourite stars lead you by the hand into deeper waters.'

Will himself said about *Winter Passing* years later in an interview with Backstage: '*Winter Passing* was so early on; I was still on *SNL*, and I think it was in one city when it finally got released. It's a really nice film. Then there was a long gap and *Stranger than Fiction* came along. That was one of those scripts that everyone was going after and I got lucky that the director, Marc Forster, wanted to go with a comedian who could hopefully play the drama, as opposed to the other way around.' It was a bold move for Will and showed that he had an eye on being in this game for the long haul and was interested in trying out other types of roles.

Next up was Will attempting to position himself as a romantic leading man. It would be an ill-fated movie decision. He starred in *Bewitched*, a big-screen adaptation of the famed sixties TV show which featured a beautiful witch attempting to oversee domestic duties.

The plot is described thus in the film's production notes: 'Out in California's San Fernando Valley, Isabel (Nicole Kidman), is trying to reinvent herself. A naive, good-natured witch, she is determined to disavow her supernatural powers and lead a "normal life". At the same time, across town, Jack Wyatt (Will Ferrell), a tall, charming actor is trying to get his career back on track. He sets his sights on an updated version of the beloved 1960s situation comedy *Bewitched*, reconceived as a starring vehicle for himself in the role of the mere-mortal Darrin. Fate steps in when Jack accidentally runs into Isabel. He is immediately attracted to her and her nose, which bears an uncanny resemblance to the nose of Elizabeth Montgomery, who played Samantha in the original TV version of *Bewitched*. He becomes convinced she could play the witch Samantha in his new series. Isabel is also taken with Jack, seeing him as the quintessential mortal man with whom she can settle down and lead the normal life she so desires. It turns out they're both right – but in ways neither of them ever imagined.'

It was a bold modern take on a famed sitcom, one that was devised by Nora Ephron, the veteran comedy writer and director behind classic comedies *Sleepless in Seattle*, *You've Got Mail* and *When Harry Met Sally*. Ephron recalled to Hollywood.com how she landed the job: 'The truth is that when I got this momentous telephone call from Columbia Pictures saying "Help! We're about to have a meeting with Nicole Kidman and she wants to do *Bewitched* and we have no plot, and you have until 11 o'clock tomorrow morning to think of something," the instant thing I thought of was not Nicole Kidman but Elizabeth Montgomery's nose, and how Nicole has the same nose. And I think if Amy Pascal had called me and said "We want to do *Bewitched*, can you think of a plot?" I'm not sure I would've come up with one. But the nose thing was, for me, everything, because I felt "Wouldn't it be funny to cast her as someone who gets cast in *Bewitched* solely because of her resemblance to the nose, this disembodied nose." And everything sort of came from that very quickly.'

Kidman was keen to star in a new version of the sitcom, but it was Nora's idea that sparked interest in the famed Australian actress. Ephron said in the film's production notes: 'I told her this basic idea of a witch in 2005 who is cast in a remake of the television show purely on the grounds that she looks exactly like Elizabeth Montgomery and would be no competition for the guy who is the lead in the show because he doesn't really want an equal relationship with an actress. That was the beginning of it.' Producer Lucy Fisher added: 'We always knew we didn't want to slavishly imitate the 1960s style of the show. We didn't just want to do a remake with movie stars. That would have been too much of a retread and creatively unambitious. What we did want to do, however, is somehow pay tribute to the essence of the show, though in a more modern, edgy context. Nora has managed to keep all the aspects people loved about the series while also taking the film in a new direction.'

Despite the new take on the material, Ephron was a fan of the TV show, and did slavish research for the film. She said: 'I watched a lot of *Bewitched* episodes and started to figure out how to actually make it work as a movie. What makes the series feel contemporary, even though it is an old-fashioned TV show, is that it's about the balance of power between a man and a woman, and that's always worth exploring. It did have certain elements that were specific to the period. Samantha didn't have a job and she used most of her powers to do dishes and things of that sort. But underneath, the show was still about a couple with a very strong connection and their ability to deal with one another given the fact that she was a powerful human being.'

While Will's casting as the male lead in the film may have raised a few eyebrows, Nora knew she had her man, telling Hollywood.com: 'When Will's name came up, I met him and then he went to meet Nicole, and it was just a sight gag, the two of them together, because he was dressed in unbelievably baggy plaid Bermuda shorts and this sort of baggy shirt, and the boats that are his shoes. And Nicole, who was in *The Stepford Wives*, received him in an all-red dressing room at Astoria Studio where she was wearing a white cashmere pencil skirt and a white cashmere top with this blonde hair and the perfect makeup. And I said later it was like watching an orchid meet a houseplant. And they were so different and so great together, so instantly adorable together – they loved one another. He was kind of just staring, because she is so astonishingly beautiful.'

She added: 'You've met a lot of these women that look great on screen, and you see them in real life and they still look good, but it isn't like this thing, where she just seems as if she's got a light on her all the time. And she thought he was the funniest person. She had just seen *Old School* and I think it was great for both of them. I think she thought "I'm not going to have to worry about the comedy because he's gonna be there, and I think he must have" – I don't know. I know that Nicole gave him an unbelievable amount of courage as an actor. I think he's great in this movie and that you see both of who they really are. You see how darling she is in real life in this movie and you see what a dear person he really is. You see down to that sort of Will Ferrell, the Will Ferrell who everybody knows and wants to work with. So it wasn't that hard. He's like Tom Hanks. He's great, and he will commit, totally. I think he's just one of the funniest men on the planet.'

Despite the pedigree on offer, the film wasn't the hit many people expected it to be. *New York Magazine* wasted no time in launching a scathing rant at Will, saying: 'Oh, let's just cut to the chase here: What the hell is Will Ferrell doing to his career? After *Old School* and *Elf*, it seemed as though he was going to be the new king of film comedy – he'd taken the big-boned, rangy athleticism he'd honed on *Saturday Night Live* (in, for example, his great cheerleader sketches with Cheri Oteri) and transferred them to the movies with smashing effect. With his Raisinet-size eyes and doughy face, his willingness to shuck his clothes and yell out amiably absurd non sequiturs, Ferrell was something fresh: a wild man with whom you could identify. Unlike Jerry Lewis, a previous generation's go-for-broke nut, Ferrell kept his ego in check and made himself sympathetic, not tyrannically pathetic. He could even make a vehicle like the uneven *Anchorman* enjoyable for his double-takes of quiet desperation, and you knew the flop-sweat failure of *Melinda and Melinda* was Woody Allen's, not his. So Ferrell was still poised to lock up this summer in comedy. But first came the surprisingly drab, poky soccer-dad dud

Kicking & Screaming, and now he's playing another no-win role: an unlikeable character – a vain actor named Jack Wyatt – who takes a job playing Darrin in a contemporary TV remake of *Bewitched*. By insisting that an unknown be cast opposite him in Montgomery's old Samantha role, Jack stumbles upon Kidman's Isabel, who really is a witch, but (like Samantha in the original) is trying to lay off the magic to lead a "normal" life.'

There would be several other scathing reviews, and with poor box-office sales it was seen as a dud. Will joked at a comedy show when an audience member asked: 'I just want to know why you did *Bewitched*, because it really sucked.' He replied: 'Connor, I'm not going to lie to you, that hurt me. Here's the thing: Day 1 of shooting, I said, "We're in the shitter." But I don't quit. I fulfil my contract. And while it was maybe not a popular movie here, in Portugal, I cannot leave my hotel, that film was so huge.' However, in *Premiere* Magazine, he reasoned: 'Not to say it's a perfect movie by any means, but it's definitely not as bad as what it got beat up for. I loved doing it, but for whatever reasons, it became the poster child that summer for Hollywood's inability to have original ideas.'

As mentioned above, Will also had *Kicking & Screaming* released that year – a family comedy that attempted to merge Will's frenzied shtick with a heartwarming plot of Ferrell trying to inspire a soccer team made out of plucky underdog misfits.

The plot was described by the production notes thus:

'Will Ferrell ... stars in a lively comedy about the cut-throat, hyper-competitive world ... of little league soccer. *Kicking & Screaming* stars Ferrell as Phil Weston, an average Joe who's had to put up all his life with his overly competitive father, Buck (Robert Duvall). When Phil decides to coach his 10-year-old son's soccer team, he goes head-to-head for the league championship against Buck, who coaches his own young son on the preeminent team of the league. Old scores come into play as Phil and Buck find themselves going to extreme measures to win the championship trophy. The comedy is directed by Jesse Dylan (*American Wedding*, *How High*) and is produced by Jimmy Miller (*Elf*) and Charles Roven (*Scooby-Doo 2: Monsters Unleashed*); the writers are Leo Benvenuti & Steve Rudnick (*The Santa Clause*, *Space Jam*). Judd Apatow and Daniel Lupi serve as executive producers.'

Every film has an origin, a spark that grows from a mind and develops into a movie. This particular spark began between a conversation with Will and his producer friend Jimmy Miller. Said Miller: 'Will had done a sketch on *Saturday Night Live* where he ended up berating this little boy – and it was very funny – especially because of the visual of Will being so much physically bigger. We thought anything he'd do with kids had great comic potential.' He added: 'Will and I wanted to find something where he'd be both lovable and kind and ultimately winning with the kids, but then somewhere in there, be able to lose his stuff and get sort of, well ... crazy.' (Cinemareview.com)

Ferrell and Miller started thinking about the world of youth soccer, both immediately sparking to the popular sport as fairly untapped movie material. Whether it was chauvinistic anchormen, NASCAR drivers or overgrown elves, Will was always looking for untapped material – on this occasion coaching soccer to young kids. 'We were marvelling at the fact that on any given Saturday, in every park, there's a kids' soccer game going on,' he recalled. 'It amazed us that there hadn't been much cinematic attention paid to this national phenomenon. ... It just seemed like fertile ground for a good comedy.' Miller added: 'I know this world because it's my life on the weekends. My son Sam plays AYSO [American Youth Soccer Organisation] soccer and I've seen first-hand how seemingly civil and upstanding dads turn into animals – storming the field, getting in the ref's face, following their sons or daughters down the sidelines. To say the least, it can get pretty out of hand.' (Cinemareview.com)

The film was given extra pedigree by the appearance of Robert Duvall – an Oscar-winning actor who has starred in classic movies like *Apocalypse Now* and the *Godfather* films. The producers were surprised to get an actor of his calibre to play the competitive father, but Robert was delighted to show off his comedic chops and he was also a surprise fan of soccer. He is a huge fan, especially, surprisingly, of the Scottish game, after meeting Celtic legend Jinky Johnstone. In fact, he even produced and starred in *A Shot at Glory*, a tale of a former soccer ace, played by Ally McCoist, who helps lead a plucky lower division team into Scottish Cup glory. The team is managed by the faded soccer star's gruff father-in-law, played by Duvall, sporting a wonderfully over-the-top Scottish accent.

With a glittering CV packed with some of the most iconic movies in Hollywood history, a Scottish soccer film was an unusual entry. He told *Entertainment Time*: 'I don't know, we just hoped for the best. It didn't do that well over there [in Glasgow]. Soccer players loved it but they couldn't figure it out. So like my friend said, if you're going to do a film about the Antarctic, you don't do a world premiere in Greenland. It might do better over here, it might not. But for the fact that it doesn't have a lot of violence in it, who knows? To find a market with the soccer moms is a possibility, but the language is pretty rough for them. It's hard to predict if something will be commercial. I've never been able to figure it out. The only time I knew I was in films that I knew were going to hit was *The Godfather* and when I did *Lonesome Dove* on television. I knew those were going to be two momentous things. Other than that I can't tell.'

Asked about the appeal of working on *Kicking & Screaming*, Duvall said, 'The story was very funny and I liked my character. I'm also a big soccer fan, plus I really admire Will Ferrell's type of comic acting. It's not just rooted in shtick, it's rooted in reality. I'd done *M*A*S*H* a long time ago, but this was a different kind of comedy. I just thought it would be fun.' Ferrell said about Duvall: 'Bob's a master. He approached his role from a place of reality, as opposed to, "Gosh, wouldn't it be funny if I said or did this?" He provided a really fun contrast. For as over-the-top as my character gets, he just plays Buck very real, which makes it twice as funny.' In return, Duvall said about Will: 'Will is so in touch with himself. He acts like he would in real life, without commentary or forced behaviuor. It's made him a wonderful comedian.'

He revealed to comedian Jeff Garlin on the *Curb Your Enthusiasm* star's podcast that art really did mirror reality, admitting that he shared his character's frustration: 'I have semi-lost my shit, no, not really, but I have lost it a bit with my son for not hustling. I'm like "Magnus" and he's like "WHAT?" "The ball's right there, you can get to it." "I'M TRYING!" "Oh, never mind then." We only had one kid trying hard all the time. I'm not going to coach the kids any more, I can't take it. They don't listen. Getting a group of eight- to nine-year-old kids to listen to you is the hardest thing. In fact, my wife played college soccer, and she volunteered to help out. She's pulling drills off the internet and figuring out what we should do, and I'm like "Honey, yes, we can try out these things, but they're not going to listen to you. At all." And by the end of practice, she's like "How do you do it?" It's awful. They just get so excited. I remember one instant my kid just picked up a cone from our drills and just starts dancing around with it. Now, as a comedian I applauded it, but as a teacher I was like "Come on." But here's the crazy thing, why should we care. It should be fun. I care!!!'

Reviews weren't generally kind to the film, with critics unimpressed with the schmaltzy aspect of the film, and complaining that the movie relied too much on Ferrell to make the comedy work. *Time Out* magazine stated: 'Too formulaic to be anything more than passably entertaining, this *Bad News Bears* knockoff barely manages that, scrapping by on Ferrell's goofy charms and the sight of him and Duvall going at it over a game of Swingball.'

A.V. Club noted: 'Will Ferrell deserves most of the credit for being one of the few recent *Saturday Night Live* grads who's managed to translate a talent that's funny as free entertainment on Saturday night into material that's attractive to paying customers. It's hard to pin down what makes him work; mostly, it seems to be his willingness to throw himself into a role without looking back, whether he's playing a 70s newscaster or the cowbell player for Blue Oyster Cult. But smart choices have something to do with it, too. Not everything that Ferrell's done since *SNL* has been brilliant, but it hasn't been *Corky Romano*, either. So consider *Kicking & Screaming* a product from an alternate universe, the sort of movie Ferrell would make all the time if he didn't have the smarts to co-write *Anchorman* or steal *Old School* ... This isn't the worst setup for a kiddie comedy, but it proves that Ferrell alone can't carry a film.'

The film was something of a flop at the box office, failing to recoup its reported budget of $74 million. However, not everyone was left unimpressed. Ebert wrote: 'Will Ferrell is now a major movie star, with nine more new movies in the pipeline. I learn of his status from the industry analyst David Poland, who has crunched the numbers and come up with the "real" list of box-office heavyweights. He says the top 10 stars in terms of actual ticket sales are, in order: Will Smith, Tom Cruise, Adam Sandler, Jim Carrey, Russell Crowe, Tom Hanks, Eddie Murphy, Ben Stiller, Will Ferrell and Denzel Washington. The highest-ranking woman on the list is Reese Witherspoon, at No. 12. The list is fascinating because it sets Ferrell apart from several other recent *Saturday Night Live* alums cycling through hapless comedies; he has broken loose from the *SNL* curse that currently, for example, haunts Martin Short in *Jiminy Glick*. Ferrell plays actual characters as he did in *Elf* rather than recycled *SNL* skit creatures. In *Kicking & Screaming*, he understands that the role requires a certain vulnerability and poignancy, and although he goes berserk with all the coffee, it is kept within character. His soccer coach has an emotional arc and is not simply a cartoon.'

It had been a big year for Will, with more successes than failures. He was learning the box-office ropes, and while he knew what worked best for audiences, he was still prone to take risks and explore other types of characters.

CHAPTER ELEVEN

GETTING SERIOUS

As the narrator says in the film: 'This is a story about a man named Harold Crick ... and his wristwatch. Harold Crick was a man of infinite numbers, endless calculations and remarkably few words. And his wristwatch said even less.'

Stranger than Fiction focuses on a woman named Karen Eiffel. Played by Emma Thompson, Karen is a novelist nearing the end of the work on her latest book. However, she is struggling with one problem: how to kill off her main character, Harold Crick. In a mind-bending twist that had critics comparing it to the works of Charlie Kaufman, *Eternal Sunshine of the Spotless Mind* and *Being John Malkovich*, Harold exists in the real world and begins to realise what his 'writer' has in store for him. He is soon desperate to have her change his ending. The plotline was described thus: 'One morning, a seemingly average and generally solitary IRS [Inland Revenue Service] agent named Harold Crick begins to hear a female voice narrating his every action, thought and feeling in alarmingly precise detail. Harold's carefully controlled life is turned upside down by this narration only he can hear, and when the voice declares that Harold Crick is facing imminent death, he realises he must find out who is writing his story and persuade her to change the ending.'

The voice in Harold's head turns out to be the once celebrated, but now nearly forgotten, novelist Karen 'Kay' Eiffel, who is struggling to find an ending for what might be her best book. Her only remaining challenge is to figure out a way to kill her main character, but little does she know that Harold Crick is alive and well and inexplicably aware of her words and her plans for him. To make matters worse, Kay's publisher has dispatched a hard-nosed assistant, Penny Escher (Queen Latifah), to force Kay to finish her novel and finish off Harold Crick.

'Desperate to take control of his destiny and avoid an untimely demise, Harold seeks help from a literary theorist named Jules Hilbert (Dustin Hoffman), who suggests that Harold might be able to change his fate by turning his story from a tragedy into a comedy. Professor Hilbert suggests that Harold try to follow one of comedy's most elemental formulas: a love story between two people who hate each other. His suggestion leads Harold to initiate an unlikely romance with a free-spirited baker named Ana Pascal (Maggie Gyllenhaal). As Harold experiences true love and true life for the first time, he becomes convinced that he has escaped his fate, as his story seems to be taking on all the trappings of a comedy in which he will not, and cannot, die. But Harold is unaware that in a Karen Eiffel tragedy, the lead characters always die at exactly the moment when they have the most to live for. Harold and Kay find themselves in unexplored territory as each must weigh the value of a single human existence against what might just be an immortal work of art: a novel about life and death – and taxes.'

The film was written by a new writer named Zach Helm. The story began in 2001. Helm, then 26 years old, had the idea of a man who constantly had a narrator accompany him that only he can hear. He was already collaborating on another project with producer Lindsay Doran, and when they talked about the new project, Helm decided that the story should focus on the man hearing from the narration that he was about to die. Helm said: 'I wanted to tell the story of a man who found his life just before he lost it. There's something very poetic in the understanding of one's place in the world and the meaning of one's life, but it's far more dramatic when such under-standing occurs only days before that life ends.'

After the script was finished, it soon became hot property around Hollywood, with two executives from Mandate Pictures, Joe Drake and Nathan Kahane, eventually securing the film thanks to their dogged efforts. Doran said in the film's production notes: 'They wouldn't take no for an answer. At first it was amusing. Then it was annoying. Then it was intriguing. And then it was a deal. They really listened to our ideas and they truly understood that you can't ever compromise the intelligence of this kind of material just for the entertainment value. Or vice versa.' Ferrell said about this process: 'You know this was one of those scripts that was kind of talked about and everyone was kind of circling around it and so I was just, I don't know, there was no agenda other than wow what an amazing project and I'd love to meet with Marc and this would be fun.'

The film was directed by Marc Forster, an Academy Award nominated filmmaker. Forster said in the film's production notes, 'I saw *Stranger than Fiction* as the story of a man who's been asleep for most of his life and suddenly wakes up and realises he has very little time left and that he has to do something we all would like to do in some way – change our story. I thought it was a fantastic script, a very funny comedy with heart and soul. I'd always wanted to try something comedic, but I also try to make films that are not just entertaining, but also emotional and inspiring. I was fascinated by *Stranger than Fiction* because I think we all have a narrator in our lives. We all have inner voices in our heads that tell us what to do and how to be – and what Harold Crick discovers in the midst of these incredible events is how to escape all that and really begin to enjoy every second of his existence.'

Forster was hired after the producers saw his award-winning film *Finding Neverland*, as then unreleased. Doran said: 'I would say within the first ten minutes of watching *Finding Neverland* I felt very, very strongly that Marc should direct this movie. I'm not exaggerating. I felt such a sense of enchantment watching that film. And even though the tone is very different from *Stranger than Fiction*. I was convinced that Marc had an understanding of that magical side of life which was the key to transforming Zach's script to the screen. Marc's take on the film couldn't have been more exciting. His vision accommodated all the elements of the script – the comedy, the drama, the love story, the spiritual journey of Harold Crick – as well as the look and even the sound of the various scenes. So many directors were focused on just one aspect of the film; Marc was focused on them all.'

In a 2006 interview with DarkHorizons.com, Will revealed: 'Everyone keeps asking me, "How did you select this *Stranger than Fiction*?" And it's like believe me I wish I could have selected it, it was, you know it was really up to Lindsay and Zach and Marc and people at Mandate and everyone kind of really talked about who was out there and Marc was very frank with me. I'm not very good at the hard sell, I didn't know how to approach this. I didn't know whether to say "Look I'm gonna camp outside your house for a month until you tell me I've got the part." We just had a really kind of nice breakfast and just talked about it. We were like I don't think this is a very over-the-top thing ... We kind of had some shared beliefs in how it should be played and this and that and then he was like, so look I like you but I don't know if I have to figure out if I'm going to use a dramatic actor who I think can pull off the comedy or vice versa. And so I said well I respect that 'cause you have to figure out who's going to be the best for the type of movie you want to make and then I was lucky that he kind of decided on me, after Russell Crowe fell out.'

Forster said in the film's production notes: 'When I met Will Ferrell, I sensed a man who was very humble, very smart, very down-to-earth and very introverted – and I instantly knew he was Harold Crick. I felt very lucky because Will brought the very same vision of Harold I had in my head fully to life. He has a natural gift that allows him to do things in this film that no one has seen him do before – subtle comedy and equally subtle drama. He approached the role soulfully and yet made Harold feel like a real human being, not just a screen character. I don't believe there is anyone who could have brought all those nuances to the role.' Doran added: 'You had to have an actor in this role you'd really believe as an IRS agent, a charismatic actor who didn't feel too much like a glamorous movie star. What's wonderful about Will is that he's so completely believable in this world. In spite of all the extroversion we've seen in his other films, he really is this shy, self-effacing character, and he makes Harold so funny and so moving.'

Ferrell said to DarkHorizons.com on the appeal of the

script: 'I've had moments in my life when I've thought if I wasn't acting, if I wasn't doing what I do and I had a career in the private sector and I didn't have a family, that I do have some tendencies where I could really kind of have a monastic existence and be OK with it. You know, 'cause I think there's been times in my life, well certainly recently as things get more and more hectic and chaotic, you kind of seek refuge in having some order and also just like very simple things and so, yeah, I identified kind of right away with Harold Crick.'

Emma Thompson plays the narrator and she pre-recorded her work so that Ferrell could hear her voice through an earpiece during the scenes. Thompson said about the script in the production notes: 'It was the best script I'd read in years and years. It was one of those rare instances where you think, "Yes, absolutely, I'll do anything to serve this writing." The way in which Zach Helm created a fictional reality and a real fiction – going both ways at once – is one of the most remarkable things I've encountered. There's nothing better than a combination of serious human inquiry and good gags.' In fact, according to Doran, Thompson had said yes to the part by the time she got to page 22 of the script. With a page roughly equating one minute of film time it was easy to see that she was impressed with the script. Thompson said about the character: 'Kay is borderline bonkers. She has this bizarre and disgusting habit of putting out her cigarettes with a saliva-moistened tissue. She can't figure out how to kill her main character so she spends her days imagining all manner of death and destruction. You could say we meet her right at the end of her tether.'

Maggie Gyllenhaal plays the love interest in the film, and she said about working with Ferrell in the production notes: 'Will was constantly surprising me. He would just do little things that would take me off my track, which is exactly what you want when you're acting. There's a lot of life to him and I found that intoxicating.' Famed actor Dustin Hoffman added his recollections of Ferrell: 'He wasn't what I expected. I thought he'd do comic routines. On the first day of shooting I couldn't believe he said things like "Gee" and "Golly" between scenes. He was very shy and totally guileless. But after a while I told the director, "He's working very subtly. Do you see what he's doing? He's more real than I am, but I'm supposed to be the realism character. He's showing me up."'

Ferrell told HamptonRoads.com: 'I'd show up every day and do scenes with Emma Thompson and Dustin Hoffman or Maggie Gyllenhaal – like running a marathon with all the Olympic champions. Dustin was, like, my second director, more so than the real director, who was like a Swiss phantom. He never said anything. I'd ask him, "Is this going OK? Is this what you want? You haven't said anything since yesterday."' Ferrell added about Hoffman to *Premiere*: 'Dustin was the nicest guy, and still so energetic. The first day, there's a walk and talk thing in a gym, and he had all the dialogue. I'm just going, "Well, yes." And he did the first take of it, and he turned to me and said, "How was that. Was it OK? I can do better." I said, no it seemed good. It seemed really good. But it was so sweet that he let me in that way.'

Despite the film's credentials, it received a mixed response from critics. The *Guardian* noted: 'Screenwriter Zach Helm's comedy has some quirky points, but it's very sugary and sentimental, and feeble compared to the work of those who have done the same sort of thing better: Woody Allen or Charlie Kaufman. Will Ferrell plays the movie with a look of glazed shock, and I guess if I heard Emma Thompson wittering away in my head, I'd have a look of glazed shock too. Ferrell and Thompson are such distinctive performers; a little of them goes a long way. Director Marc Forster keeps the pair within bounds, although Thompson's role demands many cutesy mannerisms denoting distracted writerliness and droll detachment, of which she makes a fair-sized meal.'

And *Village Voice* stated: 'Once an actor gets big enough to take whatever kind of role he wants, it makes sense that the biggest stretch imaginable, given his current situation, is the part of a powerless loser. Call it a "nice" movie – a vehicle designed to subvert the very mania that gives the star his juice. *Stranger than Fiction* is Will Ferrell's nice movie in the sense that *The Truman Show* was Jim Carrey's, and it comes at roughly the same point in his career. Many minds have compared Zach Helm's zigzagging script to the work of Charlie Kaufman, whose name has become shorthand for self-reflexive gamesmanship with screenwriting convention. The difference seems obvious. Kaufman's scripts anchor their craziest conceits in something actual: the real John Malkovich, the real Chuck Barris, even the real Charlie Kaufman – not to mention real anguish and alienation. *Stranger than Fiction* merely layers whimsy upon whimsy. As written, Harold Crick is no more convincing a human being than he is an IRS agent; Kay Eiffel's writing, supposedly good enough to inspire the career-long devotion of a literature professor (Dustin Hoffmann), sounds as dully declamatory as movie-trailer narration. And yet when the actors enter Helm's artificial constructs, some small miracle happens. I don't believe that of all the songs he could use to woo the baker, the taxman would dust off Wreckless Eric's "Whole Wide World". But the way Ferrell performs it – plunking sweetly on two strings of an electric guitar in a smitten trance – rivals John Cusack holding aloft his boombox. And however absurd it seems for the baker, Ana, to fall for her sad-sack auditor – how often you wanna bet that happens? – Gyllenhaal redeems the contrivance with dizzy charm. These performances succeed where Harold fails: gaining a life independent of their author.'

However, Ebert noted: 'What a thoughtful film this is, and how thought-stirring. Marc Forster's *Stranger than Fiction* comes advertised as a romance, a comedy, a fantasy, and it is a little of all three, but it's really a fable, a "moral tale" like Eric Rohmer tells. Will Ferrell stars in another role showing that like Steve Martin and Robin Williams he has dramatic gifts to equal his comedic talent.'

Following the lukewarm box-office reception, Ferrell is

reported to have told the *Wall Street Journal*: 'I did *Stranger than Fiction* and it wasn't like the floodgates opened and I got sent a bunch of serious dramatic roles. I don't think I got sent any. I liked that movie a lot, and people recognised it as a nice piece of work. That having been said, what disappoints me is that there's still a stigma attached to the fact that a comedic actor did that role. If it was a dramatic actor, I think that movie would have been put on more of a pedestal. I say to Marc Forster, had you cast Russell Crowe you might have gotten more credit as a director. There's an absolute bias.'

In 2006 an online rumour surfaced that Will Ferrell had died from a paragliding accident. He said, 'That was creepy. That really affected me. I got a phone call from my publicist telling me that there was this report out there that I was in a hang-gliding accident. I had to make sure to call my family before they heard anything. That was probably the weirdest thing I've ever had to go through in this business.'

CHAPTER TWELVE

REVVED UP

Perhaps bruised from the disappointing reaction from *Stranger than Fiction* and previous films, *Talladega Nights* saw Will step onto more familiar territory. Not that Will saw this as a return to form.

He told *The Independent*: 'I remember when *Talladega Nights* came out, I think it was *Entertainment Weekly* that wrote "He's back!" And I thought, "What? Did I go somewhere?" And they whipped through the past year [2005] in which my films in one year were *Kicking & Screaming*, *Bewitched*, *The Wendell Baker Story*, *The Producers* and Woody Allen's *Melinda and Melinda*. And they cited that as a year that was rocky. But meanwhile *Melinda and Melinda*, that was considered – at least in a lot of stuff I read – that I held my own in a Woody Allen movie; *Kicking & Screaming* turned out to actually be a really big hit with families; *Bewitched* didn't perform I think in the way they thought it would, and it was the poster child for what's wrong with Hollywood – and yet it made domestically $125m, which still seems OK ... and then *The Producers*, which only made about $40m; but they categorised it as my movie, which I was only in maybe six scenes, for which I was nominated for a Golden Globe, so that was my bad year ... So, yeah, I survived.'

Adam McKay and Will decided to collaborate once more, and they decided to move away from the smoke-filled chauvinistic air of newsrooms and strap themselves in the also high potential comedy world of NASCAR – the preposterous testosterone-fuelled sport which is phenomenally popular in the US. Said Ferrell in the film's production notes: 'This whole thing was actually a byproduct of having a lot of difficulty getting *Anchorman* made. We knew nothing about NASCAR and every studio passed on *Anchorman* our first time around and then it really wasn't until *Old School* came out and it was the usual game of, "We always loved that script." But it was just difficult for them to wrap their heads around all of it, that it was a comedy about newsmen. We were just like, "No. Think of them as crazy characters." In commiserating over that we should just pick a topic that everyone knows about and is really accessible like NASCAR and it was like, "That's a good idea." That's kind of how it started out. Then of course we gained a little more insight after going to tracks and races and that sort of thing. But I think that in a weird kind of backwards way our ignorance about the sport allowed us to feel free about creating outlandish scenarios and characters that had we known too much might have edited us in a way. So by the time that we started learning about it we had already written a lot of it and so it enhanced what we already had.'

McKay said in the production notes: 'Will and I talked about NASCAR racing while he was making *Elf*. We were in New York City and he was set to take a break before we started work on *Anchorman*. We noticed how fascinating the world of NASCAR racing had become. It's gigantic. We weren't even huge NASCAR fans at the time, but after we started going to the track, we got swept up in the phenomenon.' Ferrell added: 'For as popular as the sport is, it didn't seem like anyone was doing a NASCAR comedy. And it just kind of popped into our heads one day, even though we knew nothing about the sport. We're big sports fans, so we knew the top drivers and that sort of thing.'

Producer Jimmy Miller took them to a NASCAR race in California, and soon they were in love. 'As soon as we heard the roar of the engines, we knew there was something here to make a movie about. The crowd was huge – like a city, with campers and bonfires outside of every race. I was told that during the Talladega Race [the UAW-Ford 500 at the Talladega Superspeedway] each year, the speedway becomes the second largest city in Alabama.' Ferrell, despite his background in sports, had never been to a race before. 'I knew a fair amount about NASCAR just because it had grown in popularity,' he said. 'I knew some of the top drivers and had a fairly good working knowledge of the sport. But I never understood the intensity of it all until we started writing the character of Ricky Bobby. The challenge for us became writing a movie that was both a comedy and a racing film, because we really wanted the audience to experience the amazing visceral reaction we had had while watching these cars fly around the track at 200 miles per hour.'

Will began to test out voices for the character, and as soon as he hit the southern twang McKay was hooked, muttering that it looked like their next two years would be dominated by race cars.

Given this very male-dominated and hugely serious sports event, it would have been understandable for the NASCAR organisers to distance themselves from the possibility of a comedy skewering their beloved sport. But it was the opposite. Judd Apatow said in the production notes: 'We were very lucky to get NASCAR involved in the movie. We showed them the script early and hoped they would come onboard. If they didn't, we would have to come up with a new racing league. But they got it and we were excited that NASCAR could have a sense of humour about it and really allowed us to be a part of their world. During filming, occasionally some guy at NASCAR would pitch us a better joke than we had, and then we were embarrassed that they could ride cars at 150 miles per hour and be funnier than us.'

The plot was described in the production notes: 'Ricky Bobby (Will Ferrell) has always dreamed of driving fast – real fast – like his father, Reese Bobby (Gary Cole), who left the family to pursue his racing dreams. Early on, Ricky's mother, Lucy Bobby (Jane Lynch) worried that her boy was also destined to end up as a professional daredevil on wheels. Ricky Bobby first enters the racing arena as a "jackman" for slovenly driver Terry Cheveaux (Adam McKay) and accidentally gets his big break behind the wheel when Cheveaux makes an unscheduled pit stop during a race to gorge on a chicken sandwich. Ricky jumps into the car and ... so begins the ballad of Ricky Bobby.

'Ricky quickly becomes one of NASCAR's top stars, supported by his pit boys – the impressively large crew chief Lucius Washington (Michael Clarke Duncan), a trio of lovably moronic but loyal crew members, Herschell (David Koechner), Kyle (Ian Roberts) and Glenn (Jack McBrayer), as well as racing partner and boyhood best friend, Cal Naughton, Jr. (John C. Reilly). They are all part of the Dennit Racing team, headed by wealthy Dennit Senior (Pat Hingle) and his petulant son, Dennit Junior (Greg Germann), whose jealousy of Ricky Bobby increases with every victory. In a short time, Ricky Bobby is on top of the world. He has everything a championship NASCAR driver could ever want – a gorgeous wife, Carley (Leslie Bibb), a lakeside mansion, two hell-raising sons, Walker (Houston Tumlin) and Texas Ranger (Grayson Russell), huge sponsor endorsements and a string of victories from Daytona to Darlington. Ricky Bobby's "win at all costs" approach has made him a national hero. But as he quickly realises, in racing, as in life, you have to watch out for the curves.

'After a frightening crash sends Ricky Bobby to the hospital, he loses his nerve and falls on hard times. When his career and his wife are taken over by his friend Cal, Ricky Bobby turns his back on racing and takes his sons back to his small hometown to live with his mother. But Ricky just isn't cut out for the slow life away from the race track and soon hits rock bottom. His mother reluctantly turns to the only person she can think of to help her son – his estranged father Reese Bobby. His old man still has a few old racing tricks to help Ricky conquer his fear of driving. Ricky Bobby will do anything to find a way back to the top, no matter how many speed bumps life throws his way.'

Sacha Baron Cohen stars in the movie as Ricky Bobby's driving nemesis – a flamboyant French driver whose eccentric European 'way' jars with Ricky's Midwest traditions. Sacha said in the production notes: 'I think how Adam and Will work is brilliant. Will is such an amazing improviser. He has the ability to take any scene in a totally different direction. He's so earnest and always so in character that it is incredibly easy to improvise with him.' Will had met Sacha before he broke through with

Borat, and he admitted: 'I just saw his new movie *Borat* yesterday. He's really taken that concept to the next level. It's so good it was slightly depressing. Not slightly, actually. I was like, upset when I walked out. I'm just thankful we're coming out before it.'

He added to About Movies.com: 'A lot of the basic setup of how that character was written, and then what we usually like to do is just take a week of rehearsals to work on the scenes. We improvise them and kind of put that on tape, and try to go back and film all the options that we thought of in an improvisational setting. And of course we just kind of let Sacha run with it. We almost have to warn a lot of the cast members. In some way it looks like a wonderful opportunity, though a lot of actors are intimidated by it. "What am I supposed to say now? What if it's not funny?" We're like, "Don't worry. It doesn't have to be funny. If it happens, it happens. We still have our script here." So it can be a hard thing to let go of, but this cast was really open to doing that.' We were really, as we were writing it were like, "Who's going to be the villain?" First it was Cal [Johnson's] character that was going to be my arch-nemesis and this, that and the other. Then we started making Cal more of a buddy and it was like, "What would be the one thing that would be a real threat to this world? Maybe it's someone who is Formula One? Oh, that's good and it makes sense on a sports level. What about making him from France and he's gay? OK. I think that covers it." So that was all thought of ahead of time.'

Joining the film was John C. Reilly as Ron's faithful number two. Reilly was better known for his dramatic work like *Boogie Nights*, but *Talladega Nights* showcased a whole new side to him. McKay said about Reilly in the production notes: 'We had actually offered John a part in *Anchorman*, but he couldn't take it because he had committed to working with Martin Scorsese on *The Aviator*. He was so funny, he blew us away. So when we wrote this film, we knew we had to find a role for him. He is incredible, a revelation. We were amazed at how well he did with improvisation.'

Reilly said in the production notes: 'Will and I have known each other for about six years now. I met him through my friend Molly Shannon and we just hit it off right away. That friendship bled into the relationship in the movie, I guess. I was almost in *Anchorman* but I was shooting another movie at the time, so I couldn't do it. That was a real heartbreak for me because I thought that was the chance to work with Will and Adam. Lo and behold, they put this together and called me. So it worked out good, I thought.' He went on: 'I have real genuine affection for Will. We're really good friends, besides any kind of like professional relationship. Just as guys, we really like each other and we share a sense of humour. ... He's a really down-to-earth guy, very real. As successful as he's gotten, none of that has gone to his head.'

Talladega Nights is, like many Ferrell films, packed with improvisation. 'A lot of times it just hits me like a ton of bricks the absurdity of what we're doing or what we're saying and that'll be when I lose it,' said Will. 'But it's hard to kind of make me break. And then also, if you're really enjoying the other actors that you're working with it almost heals itself, but for the most part I don't normally have a problem with that.' (CinemaBlend, 30.7.2006) Reilly added: 'There was a lot – *a lot*. I mean, when I say that, sometimes it sounds to me like the director didn't have as much to do with making the movie. But the fact is, because of Adam's background in improv, he was guiding all the improv. And Adam and Will wrote the script together, so it wasn't like we were going to offend the screenwriter by throwing out the script. They wrote it, so it was their voice and they were the authority about what it should be. The script was very good. It was very funny, very tightly written. It wasn't like, "This is a mess. Let's make something up."' (About.com Hollywood Movies)

Reilly continued: 'What happens is you get talented people involved and everyone shows up on the day. The script is great and you do that a couple of times and all of the sudden it's like ideas just start popping up. The funny thing that's in the script reminds me of another funny thing, or what's the next step we could take this idea to and Adam was encouraging us. I was like, "I don't know; I'm just trying to get my feet here. How far do I go? This is pretty crazy, some of the stuff we're doing." He was like, "Don't worry. Don't worry." It was like the wide net theory. You just give as much as you can because we can always take it out. But if you don't go there, we've got nowhere to come back from.' And he added further: 'I've seen the movie about five times now. I went to all the test screenings as they went along, for that very reason, because I knew there was enough material out there that he could have made three movies with the amount of stuff that we shot – with the blooper reel and all that. We didn't have dailies on this movie because we were moving too fast to really watch them. Occasionally we would watch stuff at lunch to see where things were going. But I wanted to see what people came up with, and I knew that if I didn't go to all the test screenings, some of that stuff just might go away forever. Although with DVD, it's almost like that's part of the plan. You can have all the extra stuff for the DVD.'

As well as Reilly, Leslie Bibb was another surprise for a comedy. The former model played the role of Ricky Bobby's wife with so much spark. McKay said in the production notes: 'Leslie did so well improvising with Will, we immediately knew she was right for the part. But the character of Carley Bobby is a blonde bombshell, and when Leslie read for us she was dressed down and a short haircut. Once we saw her in all of her blonde glory, with the sunglasses and the tight jeans, we were shocked at her transformation. She possesses that rare combination of talents, an actress with movie star looks who can create a strong character and flow right along with all the improv around her. She is terrific.'

Bibb, in fact, had a connection to the sport. 'When I

was a kid, we went to the Daytona 500 in Florida,' she says. 'I remember my Mom getting a picture of herself with [former NASCAR champion] Richard Petty. I was dazzled by Richard and his blue car from then on. I became a pretty big racing fan after I got the part in this movie, though. Now I know all the drivers' names and their cars. Getting to work in the actual pits and garages was truly exciting and dangerous at the same time.'

Late actor Michael Clarke Duncan also starred in the film. More famous for his dramatic films like *The Green Mile*, this was a chance for him to show his comedic skills. In the film's production notes, he stated: 'I told somebody it was like being on a varsity team as a freshman and the coach says you've got to run with the starters now. When you get in there with John C. Reilly and Will Ferrell, the first couple of words may be the script. After that it's whatever they feel like doing. ... The hospital scene, all of that was not scripted. They just said whatever they feel and I was like – it was almost like jumping Double Dutch. You know how you're like trying to get in there? You've got to get in there. They were in it and they were going. Adam would say, "You've got to jump in." But I'm thinking I don't want to cut [anybody's] line off. I come from the background where it's like, "I'm sorry I stepped on your line. I won't do that next take." But they're like, "F the lines. Just say what you want to say. It's all like this. It's all confusion." So after about the third take I finally got it. I said, "All right,

Mike, you've just got to get in there. You just got to get in there and say something." I finally got in there and got loose with them.'

The film featured several impressively shot driving scenes, but the original plan was to avoid shooting during real-life races. But as the production crew soaked up the adrenalin-fuelled occasion, with the roar of the engines, matched and excelled by the roar of the crowd, they decided they had to have the audience experience the same excitement as on NASCAR days. McKay said: 'Our executive producer, David Householter, convinced us that we had to give it a try. He believed that you couldn't beat the production value of filming during an actual live race. There is no substitute for a track crammed with 200,000 screaming fans. It gives the film a feel that is impossible to fake. In terms of feasibility, it was absurd to have our crazy characters performing in the midst of all this real action. But we never missed a single shot. We got everything we needed during those races.'

A large part of the success when it came to delivering the breathless driving scenes was down to Oliver Wood, a veteran of action cinema, including the suspense thriller classic *The Bourne Identity*. 'Oliver is the best there is when it comes to shooting action,' said McKay in the production notes. 'He believes that each movie should be shot the way it needs to be shot. He sold me on using handheld, a rarity in comedy films. But he was right. It added energy to the shots and actually helped the comedy. Because the races look so real, you care more about what happens to the characters. The angles and cameras we came up with for the wrecks and stunts were unbelievable. It gave the movie a "big picture" feel – which is exactly what we wanted, because if you don't believe the racing, you won't believe anything else about the story either.'

Some of the actors even had a go a driving. Well, kind of! Will said: 'I loved shooting at Rockingham because it was one of the legendary Southern tracks. It's also the site of one of my most dangerous scenes when Ricky returns to racing after his debilitating wreck. He is so scared he can only get up to 25 miles per hour. All the other drivers just whiz past him. For the shot, I was actually being towed while the other cars passed me at 150 miles an hour.' McKay said: 'As soon as we heard those engines roar, we all turned into terrified chickens. When we got to drive, though it was exhilarating taking the curves and banking at a 45 degree angle. It was like climbing a wall – truly insane, because they tell you to accelerate into the bank, but your natural instinct is to slow down. The experience really came in handy when it actually came time to suit up and film the actual scenes on the track, as well as in the garages and the pits.'

Unsurprisingly, their experience on NASCAR has now made them massive fans of the sport: 'I watch all the races now on Sunday. I know all the drivers and their cars. I think that once you've experienced the spectacle of NASCAR racing, with all of its strategy and mechanics, you can't help but become a fan. There is a part of me that will always be hooked,' revealed McKay.

The film has the same absurdist humour of *Anchorman*, if slightly more grounded. Once again, Ferrell perfected the cocky bluster and swagger of a self-important man, as well as imbuing a touch of vulnerability – much like how he played President Bush. It was well-liked by Frat Pack audiences, who were desperate to see Will hitting the same sort of absurdist highs as in *Anchorman*. While it may not have hit the same surreal heights, there are still many, many moments of comedic brilliance, and it cemented the feeling that the McKay/Ferrell collaboration offered something unique to cinema audiences. They responded by turning up in droves. *Talladega Nights* scored nearly $50 million at the US box office, and topped the film charts. It was the second biggest opening ever for an original comedy, behind Jim Carrey's *Bruce Almighty*. It was Will's biggest ever box-office opening weekend.

Total Film gave it a perfect five-star rating, with the following verdict: 'Forget the recent blips; Ferrell is back in freewheeling form. More than just the year's funniest film, *Talladega Nights* is one of the films of the year.' *Time* Magazine said: 'It's difficult to guess who Will Ferrell is channeling here. Is he supposed to be a mix between Dale Earnhardt and George Bush? An egomaniacal racing superstar? The boy who never grew up? Just your average Joe? What's even more difficult is pinning down what kind of a comedy he's starring in. Is this a comedy about racing? About two best friends? A dysfunctional family? About an arrogant celebrity who goes from top dog to loser, and then back again? And what's with the 30-second Applebee's commercial? It's this unpredictability, this sense of mayhem and inventiveness, that keeps *Talladega Nights: The Ballad of Ricky Bobby* on track and always gaining momentum. That – and director Adam McKay's skill in mixing up Ferrell's shtick with a strong supporting cast, keeping the vehicle from bogging down amid Ricky Bobby's immature tirades and boyish antics.'

While the BBC noted: 'It's hard to get a handle on Will Ferrell. There are times when he seems a perfect candidate for the "new Peter Sellers" crown that Mike Myers has been trying to claim for so long. In his best films – and this is certainly one of them – Ferrell embarks on flights of dizzying fantasy that can leave an audience helpless with laughter. But he misses the mark as often as he hits it.' The review also stated: 'Much like its star, *Talladega Nights* is erratic, infuriating and very, very funny.'

During the promotional trail for the movie, Will announced on 27 July 2006 on *The Tonight Show with Jay Leno* that he and his wife were expecting their second child. When asked by the host if he was the father, Will replied: 'I'm not the father. Chuck Norris is the dad – we're so excited about that.' Joking aside, Will had met the woman of his dreams. When talking about his marriage proposal, he said: 'It started serious but ended up comedic. I took her to this beach where we had had one of our first dates. She wanted none of it. She was like, "The beach is creepy at night." I was like, "Shut up, this is supposed to be really romantic." I was trying to think of what I was going to say and it just turned into, "So I, uh, really like you and, uh, anyway—" Then I went down to a knee – at least I think I did – and proposed. So it was kind of funny, but not on purpose.'

CHAPTER THIRTEEN

REBOOT CAMP

While Ferrell was becoming a star on the big screen, he was also making a splash on the small screen – and we're not talking about TV.

Ferrell and McKay launched the website Funny or Die in April 2007. Judd Apatow later teamed up months later to become a partner. The site would feature original material from Ferrell and Co., as well as other Hollywood big names – but would also feature original material from wannabe comedy stars. It was initially founded by McKay, Ferrell and Chris Henchy, producer on *Entourage*.

During the nineties McKay had been filming video shorts, but as he told the *Chicago Tribune*: 'There was no place to put them. There was no outlet. We made them anyway. It was like an animal instinct. A group of us stuck together, Matt Besser, Horatio Sanz, Ian Roberts. It was as if everyone's collective [subconscious] knew the Internet was coming. We would show them in the lobby before (UCB [Upright Citizens Brigade comedy theatre]) shows. The first video was about a bunch of us coming back from a party. We were in a car, which speaks to how little we knew what we were doing – shooting in cars is the worst. One of us kept doing a Jack Nicholson impression, then kept doing it, until we're like, "Hey, really, stop it." That turns into a fight.'

So the idea of a one-stop website that was there to tickle the funnybones appealed to them. However, McKay and Ferrell still had to be convinced: 'Ferrell and I still had the dot-com collapse in our heads. The hype around it had gotten so dumb. But the guy who brought the idea to us, Mark Kvamme (of the venture capital firm Sequoia Capital), he had already adjusted. He knew you didn't launch a site like this the way you might have in 1998. It boiled down to, what do we have to lose? None of us, me or Will or Chris, put our money into it. Worst-case scenario, we have an outlet for the stuff we did on *SNL* and it gets 50,000 hits a month. If it was a failure, it wouldn't be a hyped failure. Which is what resonated. It was clearly for the fun of it, and people liked the spontaneity of it.' Mark Kvamme pitched it as a funny version of hotornot.com – where users could vote on whether they liked what they saw or not. McKay remembered: 'We weren't buying it. We were like "Don't they remember the late 90s, where it was like "That's it!

We're all going to live on the Internet!"' However, they finally agreed. Said Ferrell: 'We figured if it didn't work, it would just disappear into cyberspace and no one would ever know.' Apatow said, 'Adam and Will and myself have been friends for many years, and we thought this would be the perfect opportunity to create a situation where the friendship could not survive.'

The site says: 'Funny or Die is a comedy video website that combines user-generated content with original, exclusive content. The site is a place where celebrities, established and up-and-coming comedians and regular users can all put up stuff they think is funny. At the same time, the site hopes to eliminate all the junk that people have to pick through to find videos. That means around here you get to vote on what videos are funny and what videos deserve to die.'

The year the site started, popular clips on the site were delivered to Verizon Wireless V CAST Video customers. Vice-president of digital media programming for Verizon, Ryan Hughes, said, 'Verizon Wireless is committed to delivering a variety of programming to our V CAST Video customers and the Funny or Die channel is a compelling entertainment choice for customers on-the-go.' 'Funny or Die is the perfect fit for mobile users so we are excited to be able to bring our videos to Verizon Wireless' V CAST Video service,' said Dick Glover, chief executive officer of Funny or Die and the Or Die Networks.

The website's first foray featured a then two-year-old

girl called Pearl. In the quickly-made sketch, McKay's daughter Pearl featured in *The Landlord*. It saw Pearl scream furious obscenities at Will, who played the bumbling tenant that was no match for the pint-sized and foul-mouthed landlord. It was filmed at Ferrell's family guesthouse during a break from Ferrell's son Magnus's third birthday. Said Ferrell: 'It was so casual – like – did you cut the cake. OK, we gotta do the thing with Pearl real quick. Then it was launched, it was mayhem. Complete mayhem.' (*Entertainment Weekly*, 28.11.2007) It became an instant viral phenomenon, and suddenly it looked like Funny or Die might be a successful comedy website – doing what so many other Hollywood comedy websites, like Dot Comedy, Steven Spielberg's Pop and SuperDelux had failed to do.

McKay said about *The Landlord* in a 2012 interview with the *Chicago Tribune*: 'My daughter was going through that phase where she repeated anything you said. My wife would speak French to her, and she would repeat it. I would say "postlapsarian epistemological" and she would repeat it. I said, "You know, Ferrell, Pearl can say anything." So we showed up at his house. My buddy, Drew Antzis, who shot it, was a masseur at the time. I know him from Chicago, from [the] iO [theatre]. He said, "I have a couple of massages scheduled. Between them, let's do it." Pearl couldn't focus, but with "Uncle Will", she calmed down. It took about 40 minutes. We didn't think much of it, beyond it being funny. We threw it on the site with no announcement, no press release. Will and

I forwarded it to friends. That was about it. Within days, Ellen DeGeneres wanted Pearl on her show. It blew up faster than anything we'd ever done.'

Suddenly, Pearl was a star, receiving film offers – while at the same time the subject of debates by talk show hosts Bill O'Reilly and Geraldo Rivera as to whether she was a child exploited by Hollywood. They used Pearl again for *Good Cop, Baby Cop*, but McKay then retired her fledgling viral career. 'It starts feeling a little creepy, riding your two-year-old daughter.' However, he said: 'There's a role in *Step Brothers*, and I said to Will, Pearl could play this. He was like "Oh, she would destroy. Four lines from her would bring the house down." Oh it would have been good!' (*Entertainment Weekly*, 26.11.2007)

The Landlord was one of the most viewed videos of all time, racking up more than 48 million hits and Funny or Die quickly established itself as the website to head to for comedy, with over 200 million views and over 30,000 videos uploaded a year. McKay said: 'At first we had one guy working part time and it was sort of mom and pop. Suddenly there were two months when it was our full-time job.' Following the success of *The Landlord*, they ended up hiring six writer/producers to manage the website and to come up with content. To supplement the website's income they also very quickly began making corporate-sponsored comedy videos. McKay said: 'We were worried. We talked about that at great length. We decided we would just separate those from the rest, the way Second City had done when it started a business unit.

With a firewall, it should be fine. The rule is, never do a video unless there's a chance to do something interesting. When this arrangement works best, it's close to TV, working with advertisers behind you. The best example is Zach Galifianakis' *Between Two Ferns* series. There's corporate money behind it. That hasn't affected the drive of it at all.' (*Entertainmen Weekly*, 26.11.2007)

On 16 April 2008, the website celebrated its first birthday. Adam said: 'We started this website as a place for us and our friends to goof around and do stuff we can't do in movies and television. It's very cool to see that people responded to that spirit. We still have no clue what we're doing, and we're working very hard to keep it that way.' (prnewswire.com, 16.4.2008) Dick Glover, CEO of Funny or Die and the Or Die Networks added: 'Funny or Die has become the premier online comedy brand. It's not only the "place to be seen" for funny people, it's also the place for comedy lovers to go on a daily basis for a comedy fix. Over the coming months we have exciting changes in store to the site's design and content. We're adding lots of new content, and types of content, to give visitors even more laughs and more reasons to return to Funny or Die on a daily basis.' (prnewswire.com, 16.4.2008) John C. Reilly and Will Ferrell teamed up several times on the site, including in December 2010 for a spoof of the surreal festive duet of Bing Crosby and David Bowie, with Ferrell taking on the Bowie role and Reilly spoofing Crosby, as they performed 'Peace on Earth' and 'The Little Drummer Boy'.

Fears that the site, like *SNL*, will become a victim of its own success seem unfounded, with McKay reasoning in 2012, 'Our marching orders are: Keep it as specific to what you think is funny as you like. But it has to be about what is going on in the world. Not politics necessarily. It has to feel relevant. When I was at *SNL*, I would constantly get in arguments, "Why aren't we more political? We're not going after Bush." Then look what happened – that Sarah Palin season, they were on fire. It was about something. When we had Paris Hilton respond to John McCain [on Funny or Die], that's when I felt our site working.' (*Chicago Tribune*, 28.4.2012)

In 2012 it launched an iPad magazine, and it announced that it would start providing in-flight entertainment for Virgin Airlines. According to an article in the *Chicago Tribune*, Funny or Die started to run at a profit in 2010.

CHAPTER FOURTEEN

SKATING ON THIN ICE

Given that the brashness of Will's *Anchorman* and *Talladega Nights* characters worked best on the big screen, it was no surprise that he dusted off his ego and got back to work – once again on a sports-themed project.

The spec script for *Blades of Glory* was bought by Red Hour Films, the production company of Ben Stiller and Stuart Cornfeld. Producer John Jacobs said: 'Originally, I took it to Ben Stiller actually. I developed a script with the Cox brothers and I took it to Ben Stiller and his company, Red Hour, with the idea of him being in it. He loved it and so did his partner, and basically that was the initial idea. So originally we were thinking Ben Stiller and Jon Heder would be a great combination together. And as it turns out, actually, I mean I couldn't possibly imagine a better combination than Will Ferrell and Jon Heder. There couldn't possibly have been better chemistry. We were very fortunate it just worked out in the best possible way.'

Stiller said in the film's production notes, 'We got sent this script, which was about the first male figure-skating team pair – these two brothers had written it, and one of them was working at a Starbucks, I think. Anyway, it was one of those scripts where you go, "Wow, I can't believe nobody's done a movie of this." It's just such a funny idea, so we decided to try to get it made.' The original idea was to have Ben star in the move, but Jacobs revealed: 'Ben was making *Night at the Museum*, a little half-a-billion-dollar movie and also this movie *Seven Day Itch*, I believe they're still calling it, with the Farrelly brothers. He also had done *Dodgeball*. He'd just done another sports movie, so that was part of the reason. He loved the movie, it was just whether he wants to do two sports movies in a row.'

Will Speck and Josh Gordon were hired to direct, buoyed by the idea that male figure skating, complete with flamboyant costumes, was ripe for comic riffing. Heder was intrigued about working with two directors on set, saying in the production notes: 'It's different but it's cool, because they kind of knew their roles. They had a system, where one guy would be about direction of the actors and the motion and the story arc and all that stuff; the other director was much more the technical director and he really kept a tight grip on the visual part of the film, the cinematography and the special effects. So, if I had a question about the character, I'd go to one director. If I had a question about how I do a move and where I go or how I exit, I'd talk to the other. It was cool.'

Ferrell said in the film's production notes: 'Yeah, that's what fascinated us. As I was in Charlotte filming [*Talladega*], my wife and I were watching figure skating, and she literally said, "Someone should make a comedy about figure skating." The next day, I get this call about this script, *Blades of Glory*, and I was like "Oh my God, that's ironic – and hilarious." So then *Semi-Pro* comes along too, and I was like, "Oh great, now I'm setting myself up for that question." But we talked about *Semi-Pro* for six years, because Scot Armstrong, who wrote *Old School*, wrote *Semi-Pro*, and we kept in touch for a while. So I knew I would have to endure that question [of making sports comedies], but that having been said, I've always wanted to do a basketball movie, especially in the 70s and in the ABA! It's something I've been fascinated with.'

They hired *Napoleon Dynamite* star Jon Heder, and then went for Ferrell as the other part of the comedy duo. Producer John Jacobs said in the film's production notes: 'You know, you never know. I mean, you never know the chemistry but they have incredible chemistry together. It's like when I did *Anger Management*. It was the same kind of cross-generational casting with a slightly [different mix] of people in their 30s and 60s. In this case, it's Will Ferrell and the kind of MTV/*Napoleon*

Dynamite generation or fans. But it worked incredibly well, just amazingly well.' Speck observes, 'Will Ferrell has been creating great characters for years, starting with *SNL* and continuing in film. He is an amazing performer who's so good at what he does that you forget that, as the saying goes, "comedy is hard".' Gordon says, 'He brings exactly the right mix to Chazz, which is part swagger and machismo, and part overgrown kid. He was really the only one we thought of in the part.'

Will added to The Writing Studio: 'Just the premise of two men skating together made me laugh. The world of figure skating just lends itself to all kinds of comic possibilities. I'm surprised no one has ever thought of making a movie about it before. [My character's] a kind of bad boy of skating and so sexy. And I do sexy very well. Plus, I get to wear little facial tattoos, which is a real perk.' His and Heder's chemistry was instantaneous. 'We met in the parking lot of Pickwick Ice Rink in Burbank. It was like, "Hey, nice to meet you." "Yeah, you too." "This should be fun, right?' "It's going to be hard, huh?" "You don't know how to skate, do you?" "No." "I don't either." "OK, I'll see you later." That was kind of it.'

Heder added, 'I was like, "I've got to lift you?"'

The plot is described thus: 'Perhaps nowhere in sports is the marriage of athleticism and grace more evident than in the arena of world champion pairs figure skating – the lifts, the jumps, the routines. The perfect score results from the perfect blend of strength and sophistication, prowess and artistry, brawn and refinement. It's an elegant world, a rarefied universe, a noble place populated by the creme de la creme of skating elite. Well, it used to be. When the macho, swaggering Chazz Michael Michaels (Will Ferrell) takes to the rink, he is the rock star of the arena, leaving a trail of thrashed ice and shrieking female fans in his wake. The only competitor who can match Michaels' scores [on the ice, that is] is the driven former child prodigy, Jimmy MacElroy (Jon Heder). Spotted as a youth executing triple lutzes on the frozen pond of an orphanage, MacElroy was whisked away to days of endless training, and now stands as the picture of poise, the personification of the highest ideals of the men's sport. Michaels and MacElroy have met in finals rounds before, but their latest head-to-head at the World Championships – when they tie for first – is more than either one can bear, and their longstanding rivalry erupts into a no-holds-barred fight. The ensuing brawl not only sets fire to the World Championship's helpless mascot, but lands both athletes in hot water: Chazz and Jimmy are called before the sport's governing board, stripped of their gold medals and banned from the sport for life.

'Now, three and a half years later, both men are still trying to find their way in a world without competitive skating. Michaels has devolved into a drunken party machine, skating as a costumed evil wizard in a kiddie ice review, and MacElroy has been banished to the shoe department of a chain sporting goods store. But then, inspiration (in the form of an over-friendly, former stalker of Jimmy's) strikes, and a loophole emerges. To skate again, all Chazz and Jimmy have to do is set aside their long-festering hatred of one another and join forces – as the first male/male figure-skating pair to compete in the history of the sport – if the sport survives, that is.'

The crew of actors underwent extensive training to make the ice skating look as realistic as possible. Ferrell said in the film's production notes: 'You don't realise how much work it takes to ice skate, because you watch it on TV and you figure, "Well, it can't be easy", even though they make it look so easy. But let me tell you, it's not easy. Jon and I trained for months and it was a big accomplishment for us just to be able to move around on the ice and look somewhat graceful.' 'Will [Arnett] grew up skating, but at the start, I had to train a couple of times a week just to get comfortable standing up on skates,' said co-star Amy Poehler. 'I have a great deal of admiration for professional skaters and how easy they make it look. That's why they have such great butts and legs, and they're in such great shape. And unlike actors, they never complain.'

Added Heder: 'The challenge of ice skating was – it was a challenge but I loved it. I really did. I was extremely excited to, you know, kind of learn a new skill. Hopefully, you know, get good at it. But when they train you, you know that you're going to come home hopefully at the end of the day with some kind of new skill and for me that's awesome because I like to rack up the skills. And ice skating is just it's a challenge because it really is, you want to get better. It takes so many like, there's so many aspects to it, balance and agility and flexibility and, but you have to have grace and pizzazz and it's like, it really is, it's athletic but you really it's you're acting at the same time. Because, as opposed to like a line-backer who just has to run, oh, I don't know what, some football players have to run or catch you know, you have to do a lot of the similar things. You have to really work the muscles and be athletic, but you are also have to be showy. You have to be showy and beautiful on the ice.' Jacobs said about Arnett, who had skated when he was younger: 'He got to the point that we didn't really need a double for him. Most of his performance he was able to do himself, which sort of blew everyone away.'

Stiller added, 'I think you look at what Will Ferrell does on the ice – skating is all about attitude. It's much less about technical, I don't even wanna say 'perfection' because it's not even that level. It's more like technical 'ability', which is, you know, not very high, but not very necessary when you have that much attitude. It's like attitude-ability. Well, if I've got a lot of attitude, I don't have to worry about my ability. So for Will Ferrell, to get out on the ice and do his thing and to see him, we call it the two 'A's,' attitude and ability. And Will's got big-A, little-A. Jon Heder's got, like, little-A, much-bigger-A on the ability. And you put it together, and you get ... like, a quadruple A.'

Costume designer Julie Weiss was tasked with giving the film the outlandish costumes. She said in the film's production notes: 'Both Will and Jon know how to wear costume. Anybody who could dress like a peacock [as Heder does in his first solo routine], complete with tail feathers, and strut around in it with such aplomb that other people wanted to try it on – that makes my job easier. And Will was so excited to get into his one-piece suit with red and orange.' Heder said, 'The peacock outfit was kind of my idea because we had seen clips and footage of other skaters, just to study and research, and Johnny Weir had this swan outfit. It was kind of a famous routine. It was very serious, but the glove was a swan. I was like, "That would be funny to do, but do it as a peacock." Skaters are very much like peacocks. It was amazing. I just remember throwing that idea out, and then the next thing I knew, she had this bejewelled glove and the eye and everything. It was like, "Wow!"'

There was a real-life scare that the film was going to be scrapped after Jon Heder broke his ankle during a practice spin shortly after filming started. Heder said, 'I was going for a spin and the toe pick was, I guess, a little too deep into the ice; I really shoved it in there. I went into a spin and my foot just really held tight. So my body kept spinning and I just kind of crumpled over on top of it. I was really hoping it was sprained. I didn't hear a crack or anything but it really did hurt. I just remember when the doctor said it's broken, we thought the movie was gone. They even told us it's gonna have to be canned. I didn't get on [the ice] right after; they gave me my time to heal. I remember thinking, "Is it gonna be weird to get back on the ice?" It was like riding a bike. I basically picked up where I last left off.' A worried Ferrell said at the time after hearing about his injury: 'Jon Heder broke his ankle a month before we started filming so there was this big talk about whether we would still do the movie or do we not. Then this whole thing was worked out where it was a relatively minor break and then if we did all the non-skating stuff, it would slowly heal. Then he had another movie commitment that he had to keep which he's filming right now, and then when he's done with that we start again in August. But he's doing great. He's back on skates.'

Ferrell feared the film might upset real-life figure skaters, but was relieved after receiving a positive response from them. Ferrell said: 'The fact that the skating community showed up was uncanny because we were expecting a lot of flak. Not only did they embrace it but they thought it was funny. Ice skaters know how hard the sport is and yet they have an incredible sense of humour about it. I think they know that there's a campy element to figure skating. It's all about the pageantry and the outfits and the flashiness. I think, at the end of the day, anybody that's associated with the sport is just happy that you're paying attention to them. Anyway, even if they were mad at us I'm not really worried about getting beat up by a figure skater, or getting cold-cocked in the back of the head by [skater] Michelle Kwan.'

The film skated to the top of the US Box office chart, scoring $33 million in three days. Dialogue from the film was used on the superstar hip hop team-up of Kanye West and Jay Z on the song 'N**gas in Paris'. Ferrell told MTV News: 'Kanye reached out to me and ... I was completely flattered when they asked if they could sample me into the song [*sic*] ... When I heard it for the first time, I just started to laugh because it felt so surreal. But I really did like the song. We were trying to film a piece that they would use on the video boards of their concert, but haven't gotten it together.' It was another US No. 1 hit for Will – cementing his movie-star status.

The *Guardian* review stated: 'Frat Pack comics Jon Heder and Will Ferrell have had some dodgy outings in the past year with, respectively, a terrible *School for Scoundrels* remake and a piece of sub-Kaufman noodling called *Stranger than Fiction*. It's a relief to see them back in this serviceably funny underdog sports movie – the kind of thing that suits them best, or suits Ferrell best, at any rate: big, broad, elaborately detailed comedy characters in the *Saturday Night Live* tradition. They play egomaniac rivals in the narcissistic world of men's figure skating, an arena of sparkly spandex costumes on the ice and foot-stamping tantrums and seething resentments backstage. ... There is a steady stream of laughs and narrative interest. *Blades* isn't quite as funny as *Zoolander* or *Dodgeball*, but it deserves a solid score from the judges.' *Empire* drily noted: 'Formula rules, as Ferrell applies his shtick to another sport. But there's enough silly spectacle and eye-popping costumes to compensate.'

The website Big Picture Big Sound raved: '*Blades of Glory* isn't a classic comedy, but it's diverting enough, thanks, for the most part, to the presence of Mr Ferrell himself. Mr Heder – destined to be known as "the guy from *Napoleon Dynamite*" – while perfectly cast in his role, continues to ride out that familiar persona that carried him through *Benchwarmers* (ick) and *School for Scoundrels* (egads). But Mr Ferrell doesn't need a great script or direction to be funny. The man just *is* funny. From his first entrance, the audience is immediately smiling. And everyone else seems to be having a great time too. Only a Will Ferrell comedy could boast star cameos like Andy Richter, Rob Corddry, William Daniels, Luke Wilson. In the world of comedy, Mr Ferrell wins the gold.'

Ferrell was back at the sports arena for his next film – *Semi-Pro*. When asked by About.com to describe his latest movie, Ferrell responded: 'It's about the ABA [American Basketball Association], which was this league in the 70s, a competing league with the NBA [National Basketball Association]. So it's a basketball comedy – *Semi-Pro*. I'm this guy Jackie Moon. I'm the player/owner/coach of the Flint Michigan Tropics. I was able to buy the team with the money from my single, my number one hit song "Love Me Sexy". The true story part of it is the NBA and the ABA merge and they only took four teams. We're trying to play for fourth place to make it to the NBA.' Ferrell added: 'It really was a renegade league in that all these guys had been passed up by the NBA. So the spirit of all these teams was that they really had something to prove to the more famous league.'

The plotline was described thus: 'In the early 1970s, there were two basketball leagues in America – while the NBA ruled the sport, the ABA was defined by its outlaw flair and sensational showmanship. Jackie Moon (Will Ferrell) is the one-hit singing sensation behind "Love Me Sexy" who relishes his role as owner, coach and power forward for the fictional Flint Michigan Tropics of the ABA. But when the NBA announces a plan to merge with the ABA and only take with them the four teams with the best records, disbanding the rest of the ABA squads forever, Moon, assisted by former NBA benchwarmer Monix (Woody Harrelson) and flamboyant Clarence "Downtown" Withers (André Benjamin), decides to rally his motley team for an unlikely eleventh-hour pursuit of acceptance and glory.'

Screenwriter Scot Armstrong had always wanted to make a story about the American Basketball Association, which lasted for nine years before it was absorbed by NBA, its high-profile rival. Scot, who co-wrote *Old School*, had struggled with getting it made, revealing: 'Whenever I pitched the idea I would hear, "It's too crazy to recreate the 70s", or "It'll be too expensive" or "Can you do a modern version?" I wanted to do a real version of the ABA, which is what makes it special.' Armstrong ultimately found supporters at New Line Cinema and the project was set in motion. For Armstrong, *Semi-Pro* is the culmination of a lifelong affection for basketball. 'As a kid I loved the ABA stuff. I even had a Dr J ball. I liked the NBA, but the ABA invented the three point line and the slam dunk. They were the funkier, cooler league and I liked them better.'

Jackie Moon is another of Will's larger-than-life characters – something Will willingly acknowledges: 'It kinda interests me in a way, directly with *Talladega Nights* and *Anchorman* 'cause we wrote those characters. *Semi-Pro* I'm just getting kind of plugged into the equation but yeah, I think it's kind of typically American like we have larger-than-life people here and larger-than-life characters in government, media, sports, everywhere. I think it's so fun to make fun of all that stuff. 'Cause at times, we are definitely the cockiest nation on Earth and that needs to be pointed out. I just love what I called unearned confidence that you'll sometimes meet someone somewhere who's talking about how great they are and they sell insurance or something you know and you're like, *what*?' (Shakefire.com)

Screenwriter Scot Armstrong first pitched the idea for *Semi-Pro* when he was in Los Angeles working on Todd Phillips's *Old School*, which Armstrong co-wrote and which co-starred Will Ferrell. As stated before, initially he couldn't find a home for the story. The production notes state: 'From 1967 to 1976, the American Basketball Association was a renegade basketball league that nipped at the heels of the NBA. Despite contributing some impressive innovations to the game and a style of play that emphasised flair and showmanship, the ABA was ultimately absorbed by its well-established competitor. Four of the ABA's most successful teams remained intact following the merger – the San Antonio Spurs, Denver Nuggets, New York Nets and Indiana Pacers.'

'I'd always kicked around the idea of doing a basketball film and I'm a big fan of the game,' said Ferrell, 'so when Scot told me he was working on an idea for a movie about an ABA team, I thought it could be a lot of fun. I'm so glad he followed through on it.' (Cinemareview.com) Scot revealed: 'There's nothing more fun as a screenwriter than writing in the voice of Will Ferrell. I'd be typing and I'd start cracking up because I'd get a picture of him doing what's written. He can do things that other people just can't do. You can write a really simple scene and he takes it to the next level. He makes you look good as a writer.'

To direct the comedy Kent Alterman was chosen, a rookie director, but a former East Coast Head of Development for Comedy Central and an Executive Vice President of Production at New Line Cinema. Alterman had his own connection to the ABA league. He was a fan of the ABA Spurs, and his family even bought a share in the team – which led to great seats to watch the team.

Ferrell noted about the different playing styles in the film's production notes: 'It was just a different style. We got acquainted with the style of play during that time. The players used a lot more straight-up defense. They didn't guard each other and they weren't as fancy with their dribble. It was a simpler game, and it was really spread out.

We were able to get these plays down so that when we started filming, we could hit the ground running.' He added: 'It was great. We had a two-week ... a two-or-three-week training camp before the start of the film ... Woody [Harrelson] was still working [on another project] but he came for the second half. André [Benjamin] threw himself ... he was already wearing the short shorts at practice. It's great we all kind of come from three different worlds, in a way. André's just getting to be an actor now and obviously comes from music; Woody, he came from comedy but he's also a fantastic dramatic actor, and the I'm kind of in-between all of that, so it was really fun to just kind of meet and kind of put all of our heads together about this.'

Talking about the authenticity, Will said in the film's notes: 'You know Kent [Alterman], our director, consulted with ... there is some guy who runs a website that's, like, everything about the ABA and I think that's where we got a lot of our logos and material. NBA owns all that stuff too so we worked with them, and I think André Benjamin had a conversation with Dr J., and then at the front of the movie we have Artis Gilmore, George Gervin and James Silas, so those guys all came back and were blown away as to how authentic and crappy everything was. So that was cool to watch those guys walk into our arena that we had made and have them go, "I feel like I'm stepping back in time here."'

The film becomes the Will Ferrell Show, and *Semi-Pro* seems to suffer from it. Ferrell doesn't seem to be as engaged in films in which he is the sole comedic talent.

Perhaps it's having no one to riff on, but he seems more comfortable when he can engage with other comedians. Tellingly, the film's highlight is when Ferrell finds himself playing poker with the considerable comedic talent of Woody Harrelson, Andy Richter and Will Arnett. He seems more relaxed and at ease, riffing with the other comedians. Ferrell is a comedy heavyweight, supremely skilled at it, but he's also very generous on screen – completely at ease allowing others to chew scenery around him. He seems to be someone that needs to be surrounded by other comedy talent, not because he needs support, but because he likes the competition element – not surprising, given his love for competitive sports.

Woody said about working with Will in the production notes: 'I really wanted to work – I should say "play" – with Will. He really keeps you on your toes. The thing I love about him is he'll never rest after a take ... he'll do something completely different. He's always working, and he's not afraid to push the boundaries of what may or may not be acceptable.' Talking about being the centre of the film, Will revealed: 'It's nice to come in and be more of the sort of support sometimes, and make an entrance and an exit in a film. And yet, I never put too much pressure on myself when I'm the central thing, just because I don't think I could handle it mentally. I haven't really thought about the implications of carrying a movie. It still has to be just a fun, weird thing.' It was the first real implication that Will's brash screen persona wouldn't find favour if the script didn't match his talent.

IGN.com stated: 'One of my colleagues recently observed that when the funniest parts of a comedy have nothing to do with the story itself, it's usually a sign that the movie isn't particularly good. Such is the case with the alternately hilarious and awful *Semi-Pro*, which qualitatively places it somewhere in the middle of Will Ferrell's comedy canon. As many jokes as there are about wide lapels, fondue and other touchstones of 1970s pop culture, most of the laughs derive from stuff that has precious little to do with anything at all. So even though most of Ferrell's comedies improve with multiple viewings, at least with yours truly, *Semi-Pro* seems destined for a short-lived celebration among the comedian's expanding repertoire.' *Empire* magazine added: 'Another lesson in how difficult it is to come up with an *Anchorman* or *Hot Rod*, and that "making up crazy stuff on the day" will only get you so far. *Semi-Pro* isn't painful, but it's a very minor credit for everyone involved.' Cinema Blend.com stated: 'It would be easy to blame the failure of *Semi-Pro* on Will Ferrell (and trust me it is a failure), after all he's already wrung this sports comedy thing dry and yet he refuses to stop doing it. He probably has it coming. I'm not going to do that though, because the movie's crash and burn has very little to do with Will, and everything to do with everyone else who seems to have no idea what to do with him or even how to write a decent comedy script, if indeed screenwriter Scot Armstrong was actually writing comedy when he first put fingers to keyboard and started typing.'

Semi-Pro wasn't as big a hit as Will's previous films, and should be marked as one to forget. And it seemed to suggest that sporting comedies with Will were getting old-hat. However, he said: 'For every person who says, I've seen you do that before, someone else will say, I love when you do that thing.' Despite his bullish mood, he did pass on several projects around that time, including a golf comedy and and a beach volleyball movie. He added: 'I also got pitched, like, "What if you're a thoroughbred jockey who's just way too tall, but you still want to do it." I'm like, "Oh, and I go against all the short jockeys?" "Yes!" I was like, "I'll keep it in mind."'

In 2007 Will was named the worst celebrity autograph signer by *Autograph* magazine. The article stated: 'What's so frustrating about Will Ferrell being the worst autograph signer this year is that he used to be so nice to fans and collectors and a great signer. What makes him so bad is that he'll taunt people asking for his autograph.' Ferrell responded: 'I don't know I got on the list. I sign a lot of autographs. I do taunt them though. I do. I really do. I'm like, "How badly do you want this autograph?" "Are you sure?" "You say you're my biggest fan, really, prove it." I'll do things like that. They have to earn it.' He joked to A.V. Club: 'I don't know how I won it. I've never been on a list like that, either positively or negatively before. God only knows, but it's probably because I punched this 8-year-old kid in the face at the airport one day, and he wanted an autograph. What I love is that the poll was conducted by *Autograph*, and there's even a quote in there, I think, that said: "It's really a shame about Will Ferrell, he used to be great, and now he actually taunts autograph-seekers." So I have no idea what I did, I don't know how I got on the list. I sign a lot of autographs.'

Also, the press reported an alleged feud with Joan Rivers – the legendary acid-tongued funny lady – who's famous for her legendary put-downs. Will clarified: 'In a magazine she said, "You have to be careful of meeting your idols, because I met that Will Ferrell and he's an asshole." This is where that comes from: At the Golden Globes, a producer told me to go say hello to Joan while she was talking to Mike Nichols and Diane Sawyer, so I do, and Joan is like, "Excuse me, do you know who you're interrupting?" and I'm like, "Yes, they're very big important people." She thought I was being a jerk.'

It was clear there was something of a backlash brewing around Will, but luckily he had a familiar face to team up with for another successful box-office outing.

CHAPTER FIFTEEN

BROTHERS IN ARMS

Will teamed up with Adam McKay again in *Step Brothers* – which also saw Will pairing off with John C. Reilly following their successful team-up on *Talladega Nights*.

The plot is summarised thus: 'Brennan Huff (Will Ferrell) is a sporadically employed 39-year-old who lives with his mother, Nancy (Mary Steenburgen). Dale Doback (John C. Reilly) is a terminally unemployed 40-year-old who lives with his father, Robert (Richard Jenkins). When Robert and Nancy marry and move in together, Brennan and Dale are forced to live with each other as stepbrothers. As their narcissism and downright aggressive laziness threaten to tear the family apart, these two middle-aged, immature, overgrown boys will orchestrate an insane, elaborate plan to bring their parents back together. To pull it off, they must form an unlikely bond that maybe, just maybe, will finally get them out of the house.'

Will said about the characters in the productio notes: 'Dale and Brennan never outgrew their adolescent ideas about what's cool, how they'd spend their time when they grew up, what they found entertaining. It was a lot of fun to explore that, thinking, What if you actually became, at 40, the guy you thought you'd be when you were 13?'

Will and Reilly struck up such a friendship on *Talladega Nights* that it was only a matter of time before they would work together again. Ferrell said: 'We sat down, had dinner, and spit-balled all these ideas.' (Cinemareview.com) McKay added: 'When we worked on *Talladega*, the funniest scenes were the ones that were loose like the Baby Jesus grace at the dinner table. That scene didn't have a lot of story directive, it was just about meeting the characters and establishing the tone. It was important to us to find an idea that, like *Talladega*, was loose enough but also had enough of an engine to drive the story along.' They brainstormed for hour upon hour trying to perfect the right storyline. They had solid ideas, but they all knew that they hadn't come up with it yet. However, inadvertently someone had sown the seeds for their next idea without even realising it. It was the next day when McKay was still thinking about an idea when he remembered something that had been discussed during their brainstorm – something about their kids and bunk-beds. Inspiration struck. 'Someone mentioned bunkbeds for their kids and I thought, "I got it." Two grown guys, still living at home, their single parents get married, and now they have to share a room.' (Cinemareview.com)

Reilly added in the production notes: 'As soon as we heard the idea, we immediately went for it. Imagine if your kids just never really matured and never left the house. I mean, I love my kids, but I really hope they grow up and move out eventually.' Judd Apatow was producer and he could see the comic aspect perfectly: 'What do you do if your kids are a mess? Richard Jenkins and Mary Steenburgen play the parents, and what's funny about their fights in the movie is that they really just don't know what to do. Interestingly, it's a pretty common problem: how do you get your kids out of the house?'

While the double act of Reilly and Ferrell was already honed, it was the role of the parents that was vital for making the film work – and it was no wonder they went for high-calibre candidates. First we had Mary Steenburgen – an Oscar-nominated actress who already had experience working with Will on *Elf*, where she played his stepmother. She joked in the production notes : 'We're trying every variation of me being Will's mother. This time, I'm his birth mother. It was an amazing experience that was just so much fun. The hardest part of this job is to get through a take without the giggles.' Ferrell added: 'In *Elf*, my character was just visiting their world, so I didn't have a lot of one-on-one contact with Mary's character. It was fun to see her perform this type of comedy. She fits so well in terms of playing the right tone.

It's a hard part: the character has to get tough while being an enabler the whole time.' Steenburgen had the time of her life on the show: 'I would not have traded places with any actress in the world. There's nowhere else I'd rather be. Every single day was a total adventure. I had no idea what was going to happen. Plus, I'm a laugh junkie and what better place to be? This is the centre of the universe for a laugh junkie. They did say that they liked to be loose on the set. To me, that was great. We do that on Larry David's show [*Curb Your Enthusiasm*], and I was with an improv group in my early years in New York.'

It was Steenburgen's presence that led to acclaimed actor Richard Jenkins signing on. 'When I heard she was doing it, I thought "Oh good, this is great." We had a lot of fun. She's there all the time for you in a scene. She's so beautiful and so funny and so sweet.' Apatow added: 'Richard Jenkins has always made us laugh and he's an actor we've always respected. He's worked with the Coen brothers and Woody Allen. He was on *Six Feet Under*. Casting him puts everyone on their game: "I better do a good job today. Richard Jenkins is here."'

It was another big hit for McKay and Ferrell, with the film storming to $100 million at the box office in America. *Empire* Magazine stated: '*Talladega Nights*, the second movie from the *SNL*-spawned creative team of Will Ferrell and Adam McKay, may have made big bucks but it was pretty disappointing, failing to capture the magic of *Anchorman*, their free-wheeling debut. But in introducing John C. Reilly as an unexpected comedic foil for Ferrell's blustering idiocy, McKay and his writing partner laid the foundations for their third movie. And if it's still a few notches beneath the inspired lunacy of Ron Burgundy and chums, it's a definite return to form.' *Time* Magazine added: 'Starting at infantile and regressing hysterically from there, *Step Brothers* flies on the comic chemistry of Will Ferrell and John C. Reilly.'

Despite the positive reviews there were several others who felt that it was a slump in form for Ferrell and McKay. And while the box office was excellent, there was still a feeling that audiences were growing tired of Will's shtick. It was important then that he chose a project that would stave off the negativity. What he needed to do was make sure he didn't attach himself to a tonally-all-over-the-place risky passion project that was big budget and marketed as a huge summer popcorn blockbuster. That would be a disaster!

CHAPTER SIXTEEN

LOST AT THE BOX OFFICE

Will was a huge fan of the 70s sci-fi show *Land of the Lost* – a goofy but thrilling boys-own adventure, which has since gone on to be a cult classic. It focused on the adventures of the Marshall family who become trapped in an alternative universe with strange, wonderful and exotic creatures.

Will was such a fan of the show that he incorporated the names of some of the Marshall family members into one of his old screen characters. Promoting the movie *Jay and Silent Bob Strike Back*, Will revealed to AintItCoolNews: 'Well, if you remember the theme song, "Marshall, Will and Holly – On a routine expedition". So it's the names of the three characters that go down in the raft and end up in the *Land of the Lost*. String it all together and what do you have? Marshal Will-en-holly.

Another thing I brought up to Kevin [Smith, director of *Jay and Silent Bob Strike Back*], which apparently was not by design, was that the director of the Bluntman and Chronic film is named Chaka, which is yet another reference to the character of Chaka from *Land of the Lost*, which I want to say was played by Clint Howard, Ron Howard's baby brother. And then there's this dinosaur imagery in the film that I can't talk about.'

When asked what it was about the show that appealed to him, he revealed to Film List: 'I liked it because it was such a break from the regiment of Saturday morning cartoons. Here was this live action show with a dad and his two kids. They had this world of dinosaurs and Sleestaks and half-man/half-ape creatures and it took itself seriously in a dark and spooky way. It was dangerous at times and you really felt that you were going on this adventure with each episode. It raised the bar to what they thought the intelligence level of a kid would be. The show didn't take it for granted and that is what I loved about it.' He added: 'When we first talked about doing it, we thought it presented a unique combination of this television show that was odd and quirky. It had this cult following, but wasn't so popular that we had to pay off every little thing. We pay homage to it but are allowed to have our own unique story. We have our own adventure film.'

To get into the adventurous spirit, Will worked on a special episode of *Man vs Wild*, joining former SAS man Bear Grylls on a hazardous trip to Northern Sweden.

Talking about how it happened, he told the website Screen Crave: 'You know, as far as I know I think my manager, who also represents Sacha Baron Cohen, is friends with the London manager who represents Sacha, who also represents Bear Grylls, and they were having lunch in London one day talking about various things and a guy goes, "By the way, Bear Grylls is a huge Will Ferrell fan, would he ever want to come on the show?" And Jimmy, who I work with and happens to be a huge *Man vs Wild* fan was like, "That is a great idea, let me talk to him", so then he pitched it to me, and I was like, "Oh my God, this is too crazy to say no to." So that's kind of how the whole thing – and then I think Universal loved it because of the cross-promotional thing and it all added up in a way that it seemed appealing to everyone.' While he was out there he knew it was going to be crazy, but he couldn't resist. They were forty miles north of the Arctic Circle, with Will recalling to Screen Crave: 'Just in the middle of nowhere, making snowshoes out of birch branches and eating reindeer eyeballs and things like that. So it was pretty intense.' He added: 'It was forty-eight hours, they scaled it back for me because he's usually out there an entire week, but they made it really safe for me, they made sure that I think I had a few more of the creature comforts that I don't think he gets.'

Brad Silberling was hired as the director of *Land of the Lost*. Will had worked with Brad's wife, Amy Brenneman, on *The Suburbans*, and he was a fan of his work. One of the concerns Will had about the movie was what sort of tone they were going for. They didn't want to make it too much of a Disney film but knew that it would have to have a family tone.

Newscaster Matt Laeur came out of it well, and Will said about his input to the website Screen Crave: 'You know what, I'm trying to think if that was in the first draft or if that was something that came around in rewrites. He might not have been, because I think the original draft that my character was on like a Charlie Rose show with a panel of like Al Gore, Stephen Hawking and myself. And Hawking starts to go after me and discredit me and then we get in this fight, I actually try to lunge at Stephen Hawking, which is really funny, great idea on paper, and then you start to make the phone calls and people are like, "No, we're unavailable." Then that became really easy with the *Today Show* [because] they were really up for it, and Matt was totally game, so that became the plan B which worked beautifully, so much so that we went back. Going back on the show is actually a re-shoot, we added that because the front part worked so great, and he was so game, he got such a kick out of it. He's already getting people on the street going, "Hey suck it." It's like a badge of honor for him.'

The film also saw him working again with Danny McBride, a comedic actor who had come to prominence with *The Foot Fist Way*, a film that Will had produced, and Danny was overjoyed, saying about Will to Movies

Online: 'Will is the greatest. I have a history with him. He was responsible for getting our little film, *The Foot Fist Way*, out there. But, this was the first time I got a chance to really work with him, and he was awesome. It was a 90-day shoot. It was a long movie, and to be stuck with Will, Anna and Jorma, they were just all great and the movie went by so fast. He's great to work with. He can make you laugh without even saying stuff. He just bears [*sic*] into you with his eyes, and you're just like, "This is going to be shit."'

They shot a teaser, with Will, cloaked in silhouette, playing the beginning of the famous song, and then saying, 'That's all I got ... Go see *Land of the Lost*.' He said: 'It was also fun to actually play a banjo for whatever the three chords I had to learn to do that. I thought that was a really smart kind of way to pay homage to the theme song by the fact that he's trying to make amends with the group with this stupid song he figured out while he was sad by himself. So I love that scene.'

Asked about a sequel, Will said to Screen Crave: 'I would love to. You never know, but I love working with Brad and this cast, it was so fun to actually work with a small cast, I've done ensemble films for so long, it was just so nice to – yeah, given the opportunity it would be fun.' But even before the film was released there was genuine fear that Universal and Relativity's $100 million comedy was going to be a flop. Days before its release it was tracking to sell between $30 and $35 million. That would have been the same sort of opening as *Step Broth*ers, but this would be poor for such a summer blockbuster.

According to a quote attributed to him, Ferrell had said: 'There's just something funny about a guy standing on a street yelling.' But nowadays Will was relying heavily on that kind of Ron Burgundyesque persona. He had it down to a fine art. However, you could feel that audiences were becoming a bit jaded. The character didn't matter now – to them it was just Will Ferrell yelling. That issue seemed to come to a head with *The Land of the Lost*. Another problem was who the film was aimed at. Kids or teenagers didn't seem interested.

Ironically, the film that would end up beating it at the box office was *Old School* director Todd Phillips' *Hangover*. It was a different kind of comedy cast, as Phillips looked to showcase a whole new breed of talent on the big screen, much as he did with *Old School*. On first sight *Hangover* didn't look likely to cause a dent in the box office. In fact, one could assume that *Hangover* was released then as counter-programming – the audience who didn't fancy blockbusters would take a look at this quirky comedy. In fact, *Land of the Lost* only made $35 million total at the US box office, and it didn't find any favour with critics.

The website SFGate said: '*Land of the Lost* was a dreadful television show. Those who watched NBC on Saturday mornings may recall its rubberised production values and stultifying dialogue, but believe me, it was even worse than you remember. (Netflix doesn't lie.)

Dreadfulness lowers the bar for any remake. The result is eight times as strange and exponentially more potty-mouthed than the original series ... That's how it usually works with Ferrell, a practitioner of self-mortifying man-boy absurdism whose exposed hairy belly is as good a metaphor as any for his shtick. If you can stand the midriff, you can stand him. The movie's wafer-thin plot is just an excuse for Ferrell, McBride and Jorma Taccone (as Chaka) to drag out the boob, dino pee and narcotic-fruit-juice jokes. Almost every gag is a notch too spacey and a minute too long.'

Empire magazine wrote: 'The problem is, it spreads itself far too thin, trying to please so many demographics that it ends up not fully satisfying any. And as it turns into a mush of uneven tones – try explaining the scene where Ferrell and McBride are tripping balls on the local narcotic to an eight-year-old – the overriding impression is of a great deal of money not terribly well spent. You can't help thinking that with a little more heart and a little less outlay it might have captured the kooky spirit of the Krofft original. As it stands, it's adequate, in the sense that *Night at the Museum* or a Big Mac are adequate. But something definitely got lost in translation.' And *Time Out* New York wrote: 'All of which should, by rights, prove unendurable, but once you realise that the movie doesn't have its act together, it somehow becomes perversely endearing. While ace production designer Bo Welch struts his stuff in the hallucinatory desert locales strewn with pop culture flotsam and jetsam, the story schleps from one cursory action set-piece to another with an almost heroic absence of conviction – playing just like some multi-million-dollar stoner gag at the studio's expense. If only it were a lot funnier, then we'd all be smiling.'

Land of the Lost was a disaster for all concerned – a black spot of the 2009 box office. But as many examples have proved, actors are generally the ones who survive. Will said in a 2013 interview: 'Well, yeah, you kind of have to do it that way because you just you really can't predict because nowadays the studios will love to kind of tell you how something's gonna do, you know, they kinda know roughly in a way, what the numbers are gonna be for the weekend and, yeah, it gets away from the joy of just making something that you think is funny and that will hopefully have some sort of shelf life because if you get kind of caught up in, "Oh it's gonna make $30 million, oh wait, it only made 22 or 23". It can make you nuts. ... and you just have to focus on just picking things that you think you're gonna enjoy working on and, or you think have a chance to work for a certain part of the audience ... so when the ones that don't work, yeah it's hard. I've been lucky in the sense that I have enough movies that people seem to really like to where if one kind of misses, it's OK, no one's coming up to me going "what happened?" 'Cause you kinda live in a bubble a little bit and you think everyone's focused on the one movie you made and people really aren't. They really kind of don't bring up the ones that didn't quite work and even the ones that are "flops". ... You just never know and you just have to kinda plough ahead and enjoy it ... any sort of movie you're working on while it's happening.'

Another project that Will was going to work on was *Sherlock Holmes*, starring alongside Sacha Baron Cohen. However, that seems to have been put on hold as Robert Downey Jr's version was also going to be made, and had more of a comedy caper approach than people expected.

Instead Ferrell made his Broadway debut, reviving one of his famous performances from *Saturday Night Live*. Writing and starring in *You're Welcome America: A Final Night with George W. Bush*, he took his acclaimed performance of the president on stage. It premiered on 1 February 2009 and ended six weeks later, taking just under $1 million. Will told Backstage.com: 'I don't know if we believed we could sustain it, either. I think our ignorance of how hard it would be was literally bliss, and somehow it worked. It all came together, with the blending of the storytelling with the real facts of what he had done, and we somehow pulled it off. Adam McKay did a great job directing and going over the script. He'd give me these great ideas, and I'd go and write them, and we'd reshape them. There was also the perfect storm of people really thirsting to see some sort of commentary on this guy. You really felt it: they wanted to have a dialogue with the President because he didn't really ever speak that much to people. But I understand the scepticism. After it aired on HBO, Megan Mullally left me a message and said, "It was, like, really good! It wasn't just thrown together! I'm sorry I didn't see it sooner!"'

When asked what his toughest performance was, he replied: 'Toughest physically was the stage show because of just doing it night after night. I thought that after two weeks of doing previews, I wouldn't be nervous any more. Then I thought after a month of doing it, I wouldn't be nervous any more. Then I thought after 64 shows, I wouldn't be nervous any more. And I was still nervous, every single night. It never went away. And yet that's why people do it, that's the tightrope of it all. Also, the isolation of just sitting alone and memorising a one-man show was tough.' (Bullz-Eye.com)

McKay, who worked on the project, said: 'That was one of those great projects where you really walk in not at all caring about what the critics are going to say, caring only about the money in the sense that you want people to come see it, but not really being concerned about that, either. I mean, that show was eight years in the making, and it just was ... the word "cathartic" is overused, but that was really a case where, God, we were able to let a lot of bad feelings go after that rough, dark eight years we went through. It just felt so good to get up there and laugh and put a frame around it. You know, the only shame of it is that ... the director of our special, Marty Callner, did an amazing job, but nothing ever matches the live experience. The people who saw it live had a totally different reaction to it, because it was just ... I mean, he was addressing the audience. It was such an intimate kind of feeling. But, yeah, that was one of my favorite things that we've done.'

It received mix reviews, with *The New York Times* stating: 'Ultimately this production is less about the legacy of George W. Bush than it is about the comic persona that has been perfected by Will Ferrell. *You're Welcome America* is a lot like Mr Ferrell's more middling movies, not quite on a level with *Blades of Glory* or *Talladega Nights*. Sometimes it's really funny, and sometimes it sort of sags. I laughed, I yawned.'

However, *Vanity Fair* said: 'Ferrell's Bush in Will Ferrell's one-man play, *You're Welcome America: A Final Night with George W. Bush*, is perhaps just what the country needs most right now – a chance to exhale, guffaw, revel in the pure comic if criminal absurdity of the Bush era. Sure, there are tangents that go on a tad too long (like most *SNL* skits), and there are certainly recurring jokes that, in typical Ferrell fashion, push the envelope of decency and veer into the realm of the gross and overly-vulgar. (But, hey, if you're a fan of Ferrell's work in such classics as *Old School* or *Talladega Nights*, you know what to expect.) Ferrell's Bush is a swaggering, petulant wise-ass; a spliff-smoking pseudo-Texan with only a limited, child-like grasp of language and politics. How easy it was to laugh at Ferrell's caricature in the early years of Bush presidency; how hard to reconcile the buffoonery with the global mess and destruction that defined his final days. For one night, though, it's a relief to give in to the dark humour of it all – the inane nick-

names, the cock-eyed cast of characters (from Cheney to
Condi), the malapropisms, lies, and manipulations. If
ever there was any argument for the therapeutic effects of
laughing to keep from crying, this is it.'

CHAPTER SEVENTEEN

A COP OUT

After such a bruising encounter with *Land of the Lost*, Will and his audience would be happy to see him teaming up with Adam McKay again. Will said, 'He's one of the most creative directors I've ever worked with. It's fun to be on set with actors who have never worked with Adam before, watching their reaction as he creates an environment where everyone feels safe.'

Speaking to to *Premiere*, he said: 'The Adam history started at *Saturday Night Live*. We were hired at the same time and started writing sketches together and shared the same comedic sensibility. We liked sitting down, taking an hour writing a sketch, and then not going back, and working really fast and kind of not judging it too much. Because *SNL* is a place where some writers would tend to spend a whole evening crafting this one sketch, and we found out whether we spent the whole night or one hour it came out about the same. I had done Lorne Michaels' film *A Night at the Roxbury*, and I owed Paramount one more. Adam I and I had talked about writing a screenplay maybe just for the fun of it, and I thought, "Let's write an original movie that's not based on an *SNL* character." And so we wrote *August Blowout* (about a car salesman) which never got made. And we said: "I love working with you, vice versa, and so let's keep going with it."'

This was the opening speech by Will's character in the script of *August Blowout* – and you can see echoes of many of Will and McKay's creations: 'Hi, I'm Jeff Tanner and I sell cars. The only thing I love more than a finely crafted American automobile is the hot rush of adrenalineI get from selling one ... Meet my car: the Ford Explorer. It's rugged, sexy and American ... like me ... And just like this bad boy, Jeff Tanner is fully tricked out with all the features ... I come with a confident handshake, an outstanding ass, a saddle in my bedroom, and except for some screw-up by J. C. Penney's, a near spotless credit report. And guess what? That's all standard ... For Jeff Tanner life is all about three things; speed, steel and gas. You think cheetahs are fast? Fuck cheetahs. My speed is American made. I'll be honest. I'm hard right now.'

McKay said about their relationship: 'We all met the same day we were hired. Koechner got hired, Ferrell, myself, another writer named Tom Gianis, and Cheri Oteri, and we all went out for beers. I always joke that

Will, when you meet him, is pretty unassuming, and I figured, "Oh, he must be the straight guy that they hired." But then at the first read-through, it was, like, "Oh, *no*, he's not the straight guy at *all*!" (Laughs) Even though Ferrell *is* a great straight man. But, yeah, to say that it was just Ferrell and me that hit it off isn't right, because everyone loved writing for Ferrell. And he's a great writer himself, so in that sense, writers really get along with him, and he's very easy to collaborate with. But we just started writing a particular type of scene together that was just kind of strange, and only Ferrell was kind of able to pull it off, performance-wise, in order to get it on the show. And we just kept loving these scenes we were writing that were so crazy, like Bill Brasky, Insane OB/GYN, Neil Diamond: Storytellers, and that kind of stuff. And, then, obviously, I wrote a lot of the Bush stuff, too. So when he started doing movies, y'know, he had an option, and he was, like, "Hey, you wanna write something with me?" And that's when we wrote the car-salesman script, *August Blowout*, and from there we just kept writing, and we wrote *Anchorman* and this other stuff. So, yeah, it's been a long time since we met in 1995.' (Bullz-Eye.com)

Their next project together would be *The Other Guys*. *The Other Guys* was described thus: 'NYPD Detectives Christopher Danson and P. K. Highsmith (Dwayne Johnson and Samuel L. Jackson) are the baddest and most beloved cops in New York City. They don't get tattoos, other men get tattoos of them. Two desks over and one back sit Detectives Allen Gamble (Will Ferrell) and Terry Hoitz (Mark Wahlberg). You've seen them in the background of photos of Danson and Highsmith, out of focus and eyes closed. They're not heroes, they're "The Other Guys". But every cop has his or her day and soon Gamble and Hoitz stumble into a seemingly innocuous case no other detective wants to touch that could turn into New York City's biggest crime. It's the opportunity of their lives, but do these guys have the right stuff?'

The little seed that every movie is grown from originated at the 2007 Academy Awards. Will Ferrell and Jack Black were performing a routine on the biggest stage. Their routine consisted of firing mock insults at the nominees, including Ferrell rasping at Ryan Gosling: 'You're all him and now, well, I'm going to break your hip. Right now.' Jack Black also got into the routine with relish – telling Peter O'Toole 'I'm going to beat you down with my Nickelodeon award.' However, when Ferrell tried to jibe with Mark Wahlberg, he jokingly began to feel intimated. 'I won't mess with you. You're actually kind of a badass. Once again, I hope we're cool. You are very talented.'

Ferrell told Entertainment Weekly: 'We thought that intensity, that unblinking menacing thing he has, put in the proper context, could be really funny. We learned on *Saturday Night Live* that it's fun to work with actors who aren't necessarily known for comedy, and just throw them into the mix, because they commit to the character and the idea.' Wahlberg revealed how he managed to land the part: 'I've been a huge fan of theirs, and they invited me to dinner and asked me if I'd be interested in working with them, and I said, "Are you kidding me?" And it was literally before they had even told me what it was about and what the part was, and I had already committed to doing it. And then they told me a little bit about it and then, of course, they went off to write the script. I just couldn't believe it.'

McKay revealed how the film came about to the website Den of Geek: 'There's always just some little small purchase point you have. In the case of *Anchorman*, it was that Will saw an interview with a 70s anchorman, talking about how sexist they were. And it was that tone of voice he loved. With *Talladega Nights*, it was the NASCAR, Bush, Red States of America. With this one, it was really a dinner with Mark Wahlberg. We went out with him, and Will and Mark sat next to each other, and Mark made us laugh all night long. He's a great guy, really funny. And I just walked away, going "you guys have to make a movie, that is one of the most interesting, odd chemistries I've ever seen, and clearly he knows how to play."

'That was the genesis of it, and just from looking at them, and based on Mark's background, I thought, well, it should probably be an action comedy. We haven't done that yet, either, and that's always exciting. And then I had that idea of the other guys – who are the guys in the desks next to the superstars. And quite honestly, it wasn't about until halfway through the whole thing that I realised that we were making a cop buddy film. It hadn't even occurred to us, because, let's face it, it's almost a kind of almost a dead genre, in a way. Really, the only good cop buddy movie in the last 10 years is *Hot Fuzz*, I would say. I can't think of any others. So all of a sudden, we were like, "Oh, my God. We're making a cop buddy film," and we actually tried as hard as we could not to have it be a spoof. But, just by virtue of it being a cop buddy film, it *is* a spoof. It's like doing a comedy that's a Western. Immediately, it's a spoof, even though you're doing everything different, or trying to change things. You know you have to hit certain beats, and it's just the way it goes. So we kind of knew that. We said, "All right. It's going to be a cop buddy film. Let's do our darnedest to make it as original and funny as we can. Probably we'll fail in some cases, and then it'll be a spoof." That's how we got into it.'

Wahlberg added to Cinema Blend: 'I have my own way of doing things and I've always been extremely sarcastic, I had to be pretty quick considering where I came from, being the youngest of nine kids. The only thing I had was my mouth, and that also got me in to trouble, but it wasn't like it was something I wasn't comfortable with, you know? The world in which the story takes place and everything is definitely in my wheelhouse. Had I been out of my element and we were doing some English period piece then maybe I wouldn't be too quick. But I certainly felt like I could hold my own in that situation.' Not everyone is suitable for improv. Will told *Empire* magazine: 'We had one actress in *Anchorman* auditions who just wouldn't do it. We said, "We'll just improvise it, if you don't mind." She replied "No, I'm not going to do that." We were like "Well, you don't have to worry about being funny, let's just play around and see if anything happens." But still she said: "No, I'm not going to do that." So for some people it's a daunting daunting thing.'

Will and Mark were close to working together on *Cop Out* – a buddy cop movie starring Bruce Willis, and Tracey Morgan wanted to freshen up the buddy movie format that had become popular thanks to films like *Lethal Weapon* and *48 Hours*. He said: 'All those old movies had drug-smuggling story lines, if you do that now, it would be quaint. Who gives a shit about guys selling drugs at this point? Crime has taken on massive proportions, destroying the Gulf of Mexico, stealing $80 billion. Stealing a billion dollars is nothing now, that's almost adorable.'

They pitched the film to the studio. There was no script, just the idea of Will and Wahlberg playing a couple of second-string cops. Will said to Entertainment Weekly : 'It was a similar situation with *Talladega Nights*. With that one, we basically just had the idea of me as a NASCAR driver, and it became a crazy bidding war.' Sony landed the movie. The working title was *The B-Team*. But there was a problem. 20th Century Fox were developing *The A-Team*. McKay said, 'Fox was not happy. We also hadn't pitched the movie to them, so they were doubly mad.' McKay claimed the studio had a legal right to block a similar title being used up to six months of its own release: 'It's amazing that you can do that, but they could. I ended up liking *The Other Guys* better anyway.'

McKay says that his challenge was to keep the set as open and free to experimentation as he could, while also keeping it grounded enough that the action sequences made sense. He is quoted on Stack Net'Obviously, we like to do silly, absurd things. *The Other Guys* is an action comedy, and I think it's just as funny as the movies we've made in the past. But it's also a bit more badass. We really tried to come up with action scenes we hadn't seen before, and I think we came up with some fantastic stuff.' McKay said about working with Samuel L. Jackson and Dwayne Johnson: 'Obviously, you could make a legit action movie with Sam and Dwayne. We kept joking, it'd be called *Critical Hour*. We'd do the movie trailer: "As the clock approaches midnight, where will you be?" For our movie, the whole premise being that the other guys replace the superstar cops, they were perfect.'

They turned to Michael Keaton for the role of the precinct's Captain Mauch. In the production notes, Keaton said: 'He's the type of guy who just wants to get to the end of his shift and call it a day, so we wanted to bring in some real-world problems with Mauch. I come from a family of cops and I know about the pensions and working 20 years and getting two kids through school, so he has a second job at Bed, Bath, and Beyond. It's tough to come from running a police precinct and then going to run the housewares section. What I decided is that his second job is not just something he has to do. It's something he loves. He's way more at home at BB&B than he is in the precinct.' And Keaton loved the experience, saying: 'I got up, I read my *Times*, I grabbed my coffee, I walked to the set. I love walking in New York. Then I started laughing, right from the time I got on set, and I finished laughing after I got back to the hotel, because I'd be thinking about everything that happened during the day. I stayed in a nice hotel, I went to bed, and I woke up and did it all over again. How great is that job?'

Wahlberg loved the experience as well, saying in the production notes: 'It's fantastic. I kept waiting for someone to say, "All right, quit screwing around," but it never happened. Whatever you want to do, whatever you want to try, is OK. Adam works completely differently from everybody else.' And co-star Eva Mendes said: 'I've been a McKay/Ferrell fan for a long time. A few years ago, the AFI [American Film Institute] asked me my opinion of the greatest movie of all time, and y'know, I could have said *The Bicycle Thief*, but I said *Anchorman*. I quote it on a daily basis.'

One of the film's standouts is Will and Mark arguing about who would win in a fight – a lion or a tuna – prompting Will to show off his random streams of consciousness in an absurdly delightful scene. Wahlberg said about the scene to Cinema Blend: 'Yeah. Well, I'm just trying to keep a straight face. He's so out of his mind, in a good way, but with every scene we did we would shoot what was on the page and then spend three or four hours just improvising and playing around. Yeah, you know, we're getting into this ridiculous argument but, like everything else that I've done, I try to play it as real as possible and stay as committed to the situation and the moment no matter how absurd it is.'

Wahlberg loved it so much, he revealed to Cinema Blend: 'All of it was memorable, we had so much fun everyday. I kept waiting for somebody to say, "Hey, cut the shit. You gotta be serious for a minute, we're actually making a movie here," and they never did that. They encouraged me to get crazier and crazier and then when I got to my craziest it was like putting gasoline on a fire. They pushed me to the next level. Probably the most memorable scenes are with me and [Will's character] Allen and Eva and with [Steve] Coogan, with Coogan in the car was a treat because it's just us being in a car, on a stage pretending to be me driving around and everybody's kind of just throwing stuff out there.'

While it was a laugh riot for most audiences, McKay tried to slip some serious content in the film – the end credits are packed with stylish graphics and startling facts about white collar crime. He told Den of Geek: 'I think I might have forgotten the world at large a little on that, because, from my perspective, when I saw them, I found them really entertaining. I thought, "Oh, these look cool!

They look kinda beautiful!" And there's a magazine in the US, *Harper*'s, and they have *Harper's Index*, which are the numbers, the stats. I've always found that to be entertaining, even though they're jaw-dropping and startling. So, when I saw it, and we played the "Pimps Don't Cry" song over it, and the "Rage Against the Machine", I thought, "Wow, these are really cool!" And then when we started getting the reaction of "Oh my God, it becomes a Michael Moore film in the credits", I was really surprised. I also thought of the financial thing as not really political. We all agree that it happened. But I underestimated the old corporate media in the United States and the right-wing media. So, yeah, we got some complaints on that, but, ultimately, I don't care. I think they're cool.'

He added: 'We were very lucky. This is going to sound like a bit of studio ass-kissing, but it's absolutely true. Sony is the coolest studio. They are really amazing. I think part of it comes from they're not an American corporation. They don't work by quite the same rules. And their studio heads have a lot of autonomy.'

It was a pleasing return of form for Will – with the film knocking Christopher Nolan's sci-fi hit *Inception* off the top spot at the US box office. However, there were fears, given the box-office beating given to *Land of the Lost*. Will's publicist said at the time: 'There's certainly a lot of perceived pressure because the last film did not do well at all. So he's under the microscope more so that he would be if he was coming off a film that made $100 million or

$200 million. It's been 14 months between the two movies, so hopefully some backlash has subsided and people are excited about the film and the publicity appearances. You hope that stuff and the word of mouth carries.' He added, 'Will had a bad misstep with *Land of the Lost*. Big deal. There are certainly other people who have had a film do poorly and rebound.' Sony distribution president Rory Bruer said at the time, 'We're in Will's sweet spot. *Land of the Lost* was more conceptual. The really get-down-and-dirty comedies that Will has been amazing for us in – whether it be *Talladega Nights* or *Step Brothers* – we've had huge success with.'

Peter Travers from *Rolling Stone* raved: 'Take a plot about two NYPD detectives who sit on the sidelines while other cops get all the shootouts and glam headlines. Kick it up a notch by casting Will Ferrell and Mark Wahlberg as the losers who stumble into the big time. Spice with giddy action from the script by Chris Henchy and director Adam McKay. Then sit back and laugh your ass off. I did. Ferrell and McKay scored with *Anchorman*, *Talladega Nights* and *Step Brothers*, and, with Henchy, they started the influential comedy website Funny or Die. That's Hall of Fame funny, right there. In *The Other Guys*, they're flying on comic helium. OK, the balloon loses altitude from time to time, but Ferrell and Wahlberg are a comic riot. Ferrell is effortlessly uproarious. And watching hardass Wahlberg, in his first starring shot at farce, shake his sillies out is not to be missed. Catch his double and triple takes when the wife Ferrell claims to be embarrassed by turns out to be crazy-sexy Eva Mendes. But there I go giving away the jokes. Don't let anyone spoil the wildly hilarious surprises. Ferrell and Wahlberg will double your fun. Guaranteed.'

The *Evening Standard* wrote: 'Clever is not funny. Stupid's funny. Determined, persistent, straight up stupid – that's funny. Strange that so many clever comedians don't know it. Or maybe they do but they don't want to look stupid. *The Other Guys* is the fourth collaboration between Will Ferrell and Adam McKay, following on from *Anchorman: The Legend of Ron Burgundy*, *Talladega Nights: The Ballad of Ricky Bobby*, and *Step Brothers*. It's a buddy cop movie, like *48 Hours*, gone a bit funny. Very, actually.' *Empire* magazine said: 'Skewers the action genre while also finding room for sheer madness. We've still yet to see the equal of Ron Burgundy, but this latest offering is a wonky yet worthy addition to the McKay/Ferrell pantheon.'

The *Independent* weren't as enthused, but noted that it had some good points: 'Will Ferrell reunites with Adam McKay, director of his most popular work (*Anchorman*, *Talladega Nights*), in a comedy-action movie that begins far more engagingly than it ends. Ferrell is partnered with Mark Wahlberg as a pair of middling cops – not the daredevil, pistol-packin' ones but "the other guys" – who suddenly get a chance to shine when they investigate a huge embezzlement scandal. As long as it sticks with the goofball riffing and the delectable parody of cop machismo by Samuel L. Jackson and Dwayne Johnson, this works up a decent head of steam. Michael Keaton as their captain is slyly amusing, and even Wahlberg, as the angry foil to Ferrell's unheroic desk jockey, shows unsuspected comic chops (his reaction on meeting the latter's "crazy hot" wife Eva Mendes is hilariously disbelieving). The laughs dry up, however, once the silly heroics kick in, the mayhem and car chases reducing it to exactly the formulaic twaddle it set out to tease.'

Will was next seen in *Megamind*. Will said about the process of being in an animated movie: 'Well, in terms of vocals, I was just trying to go for – he's this villain who, under different circumstances, could have been the good guy. He's alienated to the point where he thinks, "I might as well be evil, it's what I'm good at." Tom McGrath the director and I, we spoke about how he should be approachable and sweet, and someone you'd root for. And at the same time, I thought, his whole life and demeanour and the way he acts is based on the idea that he thinks he's very intelligent. That's where the voice came.'

Asked what his kids thought about him doing an animated comedy, he told Den of Geek: 'Well, it was interesting, because this is the first movie I've done where they have an awareness that I was in it. They couldn't decipher the fact that I was *Megamind*, and asked, "Are you in a costume?" I had to explain that it was kind of like a cartoon. It was fun. [It was] the first time they got to go to a premiere, and they got to go to France. The best part about it was, when I asked my three-year-old if he liked it, he was like, "Yeah, I really liked it." But my six-year-old, he'd seen the trailer and stuff, and he saw the movie and was laughing at the jokes. I asked him, "What did you think?", and he was like, "Oh, um … you were fine." [And I said] "Remember you were laughing at the phone and smells like a hero and all these things?", and he says, "Oh yeah, I know. You were fine." His attitude was like, "Don't ask me again, or I'll have to tell you what I really think." Tough love!' Will added: 'The oldest one is just starting to know. I think because his friends at school say, "I saw your dad." Last summer, he pulled me aside and said [adopts conspiratorial voice], "I know what you do." It was like, "Hey, buddy, let me talk to you for a second." I said, "What is it that I do?", and he said, "You're an actor." And I asked him how he felt about that, and he said, "OK. I'm fine with it."'

Director Tom McGrath said about the film: 'I heard it was about a villain who accidentally defeats his nemesis, creates a new hero to battle, and inevitably has to rise up and be the hero himself. And at the centre of it was a love story. Just with that simple pitch, I said, "Wow, that sounds really unique – to tell a story from the villain's point of view."' The film was originally conceived as live action but they decided it would work best as an animation. Producer Lara Breay observed, 'It was important to us that *Megamind* shouldn't just be a parody. There have been a few of those in the past and they haven't always been particularly successful or funny in our opinion. Besides, we love superhero movies; we would never set out to mock them. What we did want to do was take the audience's expectations – their deep knowledge of this genre from the hundreds of movies and comic books that have come before – and knowingly up-end them to create a story that would be fresh and surprising, even to fans of the genre. Nothing and no one in *Megamind* is what it first seems, and that leads to a lot of thrills and a lot of laughs.'

Director McGrath says, 'If you love superhero movies, here's an entirely new take. We have a lot of fun with all the stereotypical trappings of those films, but I feel we made something new and fresh. And telling it in 3D animation is a big advantage over live-action. When creating an animated film, we can seamlessly blend huge effects and action sequences with intimate character-driven scenes. It's all integrated. Everything in *Megamind* is in the realm of computer graphics, where you can push things a little further than you could in live-action and still be right there with the characters. In the superhero movies I see now, everything is slicked up with polycarbon fibre and airbrushed metallic costumes. If there really were superheroes in the world, though, they'd be the biggest celebrities, regardless of the shine on their gadgets.'

He said about the casting of Ferrell: 'Casting Will Ferrell was key. He has this incredible ability to play a bombastic egomaniac hell-bent on world domination in a way that makes him not only hilarious, but lovable. He shows us the vulnerability and longing that's behind the deluded buffoon, and you can't help but root for him.'

The film was another hit for Will, giving him much needed box-office relief following the *Land of the Lost* flop. But that still didn't meant he would be playing it safe.

CHAPTER EIGHTEEN

EVERYTHING MUST GO

Asked about his toughest role, Will told Backstage, 'It was *Everything Must Go*, because so much of it is me, alone on that lawn. And I had to do some things emotionally that I hadn't done before. But that's why I loved it and why the experience was so meaningful.'

Will also said: 'I really loved that experience of getting to do a straighter role, that more dramatic kind of turn. I was a fan of stuff that Jack Lemmon had done, and even Tom Hanks, who I think we all now forget totally started out in comedy. Even Bill Murray, who's one of my comedic heroes, has done such solid work in dramas now.'

Will's solid drama would be *Everything Must Go*. The plot would be described thus: 'Nick Halsey is a career salesman whose days of being on top are long gone. The same day Nick gets fired, for falling off the wagon one last time, he returns home to discover his wife has left him, changed the locks on their suburban home and dumped all his possessions out on the front yard. Faced with his life imploding, Nick puts it all on the line or more properly, on the lawn, reluctantly holding a yard sale that becomes a unique strategy for survival.'

Will said about the character to Collider: 'To me, in watching it, it never feels false in a way, which is more of an aftermath. What got me going was that it was a really well-written script. I liked that it was kind of just ... it doesn't sound appealing or exciting to describe it as grey but it was kind of just grey. There were funny moments, but then there were extremely sad stories. It's just a story and it's not trying to be any kind of movie. I loved that you couldn't fit it in a box in a way. I also loved the premise. I thought it was so unique that you take this guy and you strip him of everything. He throws all of his possessions on the front lawn and then he makes a choice to just live there as opposed to fleeing that situation. He kind of just says, "Well, screw it. This is so confounding to me. Where did my wife go and what if my credit cards don't work? What is going on? Really? Is what I did that bad?" and he just decides to sit there and say, "Screw it."'

Writer/director Dan Rush read the short story by Raymond Carver, 'Why Don't You Dance?', and knew he had found the perfect project: 'I thought I needed to write something with a great role for an actor. Here was the tale of a man whose marriage falls apart and who finds his belongings dumped out in his yard. He then rearranges the furniture on his front lawn so that he can watch television and listen to his record player. In "Why Don't You Dance?", you have a situation where everything is stripped away and you have no belongings, no friends, and in this case you have a problem as well, an alcohol problem, what do you do? And to me, I think that that's the definition of character.' Producer Marty Bowen said about the finished script: 'When I first read it, I knew immediately that this was the type of movie that Temple Hill would want to do because it goes straight to the heart of the human condition and it does it with a bit of a smile on its face.' And producer Wyck Godfrey added: 'It's an adult story, it's ultimately about a guy who has to look at his life and say: "Everything that I've done until now may be totally falling apart, what am I going to do from here?" I think we live in a time where that's happening to a lot of people, people lose their jobs all the time, people get divorced all the time and I think that's something that a lot of people can relate to.'

Bowen said to Daily News: 'Will has an inherent sympathy – there's not a mean-spirited bone in his body.' Will added (askmen.com): 'I thought it was one of the most original scripts I had ever come across as well as the challenge of doing something this serious. So I said to the director, Dan Rush, that I'd love to do this but he'd have to wait for me for a year and a half. I really have that many things lined up. And he did! So that's actually how it happened. We were very frank with him. We said,

"Understand that we think that this is so great, and we understand if you don't want to wait for us, because there must be many other actors that are clamouring to do this." But he did. He wanted to wait for me. You'll have to ask him why.'

He added in the same interview: 'I don't know if it was less pressure, but it was definitely freeing to do something like this probably because there are parts in the film that are just real life. You don't have to think what the joke's going to be, and it's OK ... There is a lot of stillness in the movie, and I think a lot of people are afraid to do those types of movies. It was really refreshing to be still in that way, as opposed to running around and acting crazy, as much as you love it, or hopefully love it. But, yes, it was very freeing. And in terms of whether this was a conscious choice to do something less comic, this was more just an individual project that kind of came my way. Since *Stranger than Fiction*, this was the only film offered to me that has been off the track of what I normally do. There is a three-to-four-year gap, so I just jumped at the chance to do it and would like to do more. But it will be another four-year gap probably. It's just the way people are conditioned to think. I think no matter how high you go up in the food chain, I think you're still typecast in a way.'

He worked for a fraction of what he normally earns, revealing: 'The thing that was really gratifying was on a $5 million movie, everyone on the cast or the crew, you knew no one was there for the money. Everyone was there because they really loved the script. You would think that on a smaller budget this experience unified everyone. It was a real team effort. And I've never experienced anything like that. It was great.'

Ferrell said about his relationship with Rebecca Hall's character in the film to Screen Crace: 'That was another thing that I loved about this script. Here was this relationship that normally, in a typical Hollywood movie, they would fall in love and it feels like it's maybe getting to that edge, but in a very real way, it never really crosses that line. It's almost symbolic of that dance at the end of the film. It really is a dance of them consoling each other, helping each other, being critical of each other too, and yet they don't cross that line of intimacy, yet there is something intimate going on between them. I just thought that was masterfully done on a script level and we tried to just be true to that.' According to Rebecca Hall it was a 'hysterical set', with the pretty actress succumbing to the thing that follows Ferrell about, constantly quoting his films back to him. Light relief on set was provided by Rebecca Hall, who challenged everyone to make a playlist that your 15-year-old self would have made if they were going on a date.

It was a challenging film for Will, and he called it one of his toughest acting experiences, telling Collider: 'It was intense, but it made the work go by pretty quickly. But there were days where I was just like, "Wow. I am exhausted." I don't know. A lot of the times you read something and you don't realise that you are going to have to do the things that you read. I remember reading *Old School* for the first time and I read the part about streaking and I was like, "Oh, that is a funny joke when that happens." Later, it hit me that night that "Oh, I actually have to do it." I'm in the movie constantly so therefore I never left the set. I would just sit out there partly because it helped to be there ready to go when we were filming. Every day was such a struggle because most of it is day-time exteriors and we are out there fighting the light. So I would just stay out on the lawn. I would look over my lines and just be in the environment of that yard. So knowing that I had to be there all the time kind of helped me stay in that zone with the character.

While he was pleased with the film, he feared that some of his fans and the film critics wouldn't be happy unless he starred in more comedy fare. He told Backstage.com: 'I do think people get shook up in a way by comedians wanting to do drama that doesn't happen in the opposite regard. When a dramatic actor does a funny film, people are like, "Wonderful! I didn't know he was funny!" But when it flips, people can get really thrown by it. But I just couldn't worry about it. When something like this comes along and it's different and a way to stretch as an actor, I have to leap. It's human nature to want to try to do different things.'

And he had plenty of varied projects to work on, telling Collider.com that he had been keeping busy and making sure the projects that he worked on were interesting: 'I think last year, maybe starting with the Bush show on

Broadway, to rolling into this year was really kind of a fun ... to call it a realisation isn't accurate. But it kind of kicked off this thing in wanting to make sure that I just keep kind of tweaking things along the way. Along with studio movies I want to keep doing ... it was just so fun. Last year, my life consisted of working on two $5 million twenty-three-day shoot films, and they were two of the most satisfying experiences that I have ever had. They were both radically different between something that is more of an acting exercise to *Casa de mi Padre*, which is just so out there. To do an entire movie in Spanish, which was another thing that was just like, "Wow. Be careful what you wish for." And then getting to do *The Office*. I think it's kind of a triumvirate of an example of how I want to just keep showing up in places that you least expect me.'

The Guardian stated: 'We initially believe that this is a black comedy for our present depressed time, the bitter flip side of *Up in the Air*, and this seems to be confirmed by the casting of star comedian Will Ferrell as Nick. The film is certainly not without humour. But Ferrell played it fairly straight in Woody Allen's *Melinda and Melinda* and Marc Forster's *Stranger than Fiction* and here his baffled, bitter alcoholic is as impressive and as tinged with tragedy as that of another fine comedian, Jack Lemmon, in *Days of Wine and Roses*. And naturally we recall Lemmon's last major screen role in Altman's *Short Cuts*.' *The Hollywood Reporter* stated: 'Will Ferrell does a serious turn in *Everything Must Go* with mixed results. Playing an alcoholic at a crucial crossroad in his life, he uses his middle-age slacker persona well to convey a guy lost in his own immaturity and low self-esteem. And he nicely finds humour in an otherwise pathetic situation. But the performance is too one-note. Using an acting muscle hitherto ignored, Ferrell isn't able to track the ups-and-downs in the story's dramatic beats. Instead he falls back on physical humour and facial expressions that don't quite get to the bottom of what ails his character.'

The *Film Journal* added: 'The film is much stronger when it resists the feel-good platitudes, as when Nick, who is generally taciturn, finally tells Samantha what he thinks of her marriage, or when it allows Farrell to exercise some of his comic skill. After Nick is fired, he stabs his boss' tyre with his going-away present, a Swiss army knife. The only problem is, he can't pull it out, and it's inscribed. It's hard watching Ferrell's hilarious execution of this early scene sensing that this will not be a funny or even particularly enjoyable movie. Farrell does, however, hold the stage, or lawn, with his surprisingly expressive face, by turns registering rage, vulnerability, stoicism and yearning. But *the Wall Street Journal* noted: 'It would be nice to report that Mr Ferrell overcomes these dramatic obstacles. He's a serious actor as well as a fine funny man. (Check out his performance as a charmingly foolish actor in Woody Allen's *Melinda and Melinda*.) But Mr Rush's film functions, for the most part, in such a narrow emotional range – from sad through mournful to lugubrious, with surprisingly few side trips to anger – that you keep rooting for its star to lighten up, which he eventually does when it's almost too late. From time to time the movie grabs you (though the music keeps repelling you). Taking stock and letting go – of superfluous things, of worn-out love – is a strong theme. But the progression of the script is like Nick's self-help programme. We're familiar with the steps.'

Will was back in risky mode once more. For the next project Will decided on something a little mainstream. Sometimes, he reckoned, it's good to get scared. *Casa de mi Padre* was an idea he had, years ago. Ferrell said: 'I don't remember when I got the idea and there was really no good reason, but I always had the notion of doing a Spanish language comedy. I do not speak Spanish but I thought the concept of having someone who is – depending on who you talk to – either fairly well-known or kind of well-known in American language film – placed in a foreign language film would be something you don't see every day. And I love the Mexican-Western genre.'

He turned to writer Andrew Steele and director Matt Piedmont – both *SNL* regulars. He added in the film's production notes: 'I just had the most general concept of what the movie would be about, but I had nothing specific and that's where Andrew Steele, a writer who is a longtime friend from our time together at *Saturday Night Live*, came in. I pitched the potential, and asked him if he thought this would be fun to write? And he actually came up with the story of *Casa de mi Padre*. And then we reached out to another friend of ours from *Saturday Night Live*, Matt Piedmont.' Said Steele: 'From the outset, Will had always framed the project as something like a telenovela. Telenovelas have always been a staple for comedy writers. When I was at *Saturday Night Live*, we probably parodied telenovelas five or six different times. They are so over the top and so dramatic that they just lend themselves to satire. We did not want to do a mere parody however, so we used the telenovela as a kind of springboard for something hopefully more imaginative, with an affectionate nod towards the format.'

Will told *Rolling Stone* about the film during a break in shooting *The Campaign* in New Orleans, telling it simply: 'I can't tell you where I first thought of *Casa de mi Padre* and I can't tell you when, but a lightbulb went off that said putting me in a Spanish-speaking movie with the cast being entirely Latino, and myself playing a kind of Latino actor, and the joke not being that I'm speaking poor Spanish, that it would be hilarious. I guess I did it specifically to raise the question "Why did you do this?" It's one of the craziest things I've done.'

It was done because he was annoyed with Hollywood, he told *The New York Times*: 'It's one of the more creatively timid times in Hollywood. You find yourself going, "If they're not going to make this movie, why don't I go off and play in this area for little or no money?"' In another interview he revealed that he pitched a story idea that he had. 'It's this wonderful story in the comedy-drama category. It's a real story about a guy who was asked to redesign the traffic light system in Baghdad once the invasion was done.' He pitched it to a venture capital firm. They ran the numbers in this weird clinical way. War movie, Will Ferrell, does not compute.' He added: 'Someone in a meeting I think expressed it: "I didn't want to go see a movie that I had to read." I think that is probably a prevailing thought with moviegoers, and with studios for sure. All the studios sat in a room and watched this, and everyone passed. So there is no question that they thought it was either too left of centre, or too something, to take a chance on. Which I was surprised by, only because you hear about how Hispanics are one of the biggest blocks of people that go to the movies, and they are always looking to grab that audience. We have a pretty well known cast, and then you have someone from comedy entering in the mix. And we did it for about $5 or $6 million, the whole thing. So I thought for sure that would be something you want to snap up and take a chance on, at least. But I guess not.'

Director Matt said: 'For Will it was surely a *Heart of Darkness* in that he pulled off something almost impossible that surely caused him night sweats: having to act in a very specific Northern Mexican accent in a language he does not speak. He is the Muhammad Ali of improv and we tied one hand behind his back and threw him to the lions covered in barbecue sauce. For me it was pure joy and a grand psychedelic trip down a crazy rabbit hole, like being strapped to a rocket ship of love made of liquid lightning.'

Will said to Contact Music: 'The script was amazing

and had everything. The fact that it was in Spanish only sealed the deal for me. You only get one first feature, and I'm thrilled mine is a Spanish language satire rated R for "sexual content, drug use and bloody violence" as stated by the MPAA [Motion Picture Association of America]. They can't take that away from me.' Ferrell added: 'This is all an homage to all my former Spanish teachers to show them that I was listening. I was paying attention. I wanted my Spanish to be as good as it could be – I didn't want the joke to just be that I was speaking bad Spanish.'

Genesis Rodriguez played Will's love interest, and she insists she was the right choice as she learned her acting trade by making the Spanish telenovelas that the film successfully parodies. She told Hollywood.com: 'Sometimes you get dialogue that you can't say because it's so unbelievable. But it's kind of fun because you get all sorts of crazy situations and it trains you. You could be blind one week and wake up and you can see. My most extreme situation was I was born with a birth defect in a soap opera, so I had a gigantic nose and buck teeth and my ears stuck out. My character goes through an extreme makeover and she changes into the villain because she's beautiful. I wish I was kidding but it really did happen. I had incredible acting challenges. I went to the University of [Latin TV soap network] Telemundo.' In another interview she recalled how it was essential to learn the lines while working on the Spanish soap operas, joking 'if you don't learn the lines, the writers kill off your character.'

The *Boston Herald* called the film a Spanish language answer to *Three Amigos*. The *Guardian* stated: 'Will Ferrell plays humble *ranchero* Armando whose simple, sweet nature is ridiculed by his landowning father and successful businessman brother, Raul (Diego Luna). When Raul returns to the ranch with a gorgeous bride to be, hearts flutter and forbidden romance blossoms against the backdrop of a war between DEA [Drug Enforcement Administration] and drug runners. *Casa* is a spoof of soapy *telenovelas*, poverty-row Westerns and over-the-border B-movies. Painted backdrops, reused rear-projection footage and intentionally bad continuity are thrown in, though never as sharp or dense as in the superior spoofery of, say, *Black Dynamite*. Ferrell couldn't look less Mexican if he tried, a decent if well-worn gag, and the dialogue is all in Spanish, subtitled but hardly needed. It's all a little undercooked, playing more like an extended version of a very funny trailer than an actual, full-bodied comedy.'

Will was happy with the risks that he was taking: 'I got to shoot *Casa* and *Everything Must Go* in the same year. Talk about two wildly different movies, and yet two of the best creative experiences I've ever had. And big chances, risks to take, but well worth it, as far as I'm concerned.' And he was beginning to let his career do what it had to: 'I'm just learning to trust that it all kind of seems to take care of itself. I think I would sweat those things out a little more when I had just left *Saturday Night Live*. But now I don't even know where this path is going, and around every bend there is a new surprise. But no, I trust that you look at projects sent to you, and you make decisions while trying to still, obviously, make mainstream movies. Those opportunities aren't dwindling in any way, so that's good.'

At the end of 2012, Will received some good news – of a sort. After topping the list of 'Most Overpaid Actor' in a survey compiled by *Forbes Magazine* for two of the previous four years, he didn't make it into the 2012 list. Talking about that list, he said: 'I think it's a badge of honour. Aren't we all striving to be overpaid for what we do? It's funny. Two years ago I was in Australia, and a journalist said, "You're on the top ten list of most bankable stars." Then all of a sudden it flips. I don't know who's doing the calculations. But now, I've had two hit movies, so maybe I'll descend the ranks into profitability again. I know how to fix the balance. I wanna be in the next *Terminator* movie, and do it for one dollar. And then it'll make a few million, and I'll be real value for money.'

CHAPTER NINETEEN

GETTING POLITICAL

While Will was starting to make really risky choices on the big screen, on the small screen he was back making audiences laugh in recurring roles on *Eastbound & Down*, *The Office* and *30 Rock*. But he would soon be back where he belonged, doing what he does best in *The Campaign*.

The production notes described the plot thus: 'When long-term congressman Cam Brady (Will Ferrell) commits a major public gaffe before an upcoming election, a pair of ultra-wealthy CEOs plot to put up a rival candidate and gain influence over their North Carolina district. Their man: Marty Huggins (Zach Galifianakis), director of the local Tourism Center. At first, Marty appears to be the unlikeliest possible choice but, with the help of his new benefactors' support, a cutthroat campaign manager and his family's political connections, he soon becomes a contender who gives the charismatic Cam plenty to worry about. As Election Day closes in, the two are locked in a dead heat, with insults quickly escalating to injury until all they care about is burying each other, in this mudslinging, back-stabbing, home-wrecking comedy from *Meet the Parents* director Jay Roach that takes today's political circus to its logical next level. Because even when you think campaign ethics have hit rock bottom, there's room to dig a whole lot deeper.'

The film was originally called *Dog Fight*, which would see the two main actors play rival politicians battling it out for a congressional set in North Carolina. The two stars also produced the movie, as did regular Ferrell collaborator Adam McKay. *Eastbound & Down*'s Shawn Harwell and Chris Henchy wrote the script. The film would once again see Ferrell work with his *Austin Powers* director Jay Roach – although this time it wouldn't be a cameo, but a starring role. While he's better known for his comedies, Roach has addressed political concerns before, but in a more serious style, in HBO dramas *Recount* and *Game Change*. However, this time he thought tickling the funny bone was the right approach – 'I think comedy is the correct response to politics these days. At least it gives you something to laugh about and makes the reality of it easier to swallow, whereas if you just watch the news it can be pretty scary. Looking at some of today's election campaigns, I don't know if this is what our founding fathers had in mind.'

He added to the Collider website: 'Well, it's kind of fun because a lot of times in comedy you want the straight version of things to be as straight as they can so the X factor can be as absurd and out there as you need it to be and to actually be, "You know what, I think in this press conference this is what would happen. Here's who would be standing there and here is how much security they would have. Here's what kind of cameras would be at this level." You know, I actually did so much research on those things for *Recount* and *Game Change* that I felt pretty confident about how to deliver a groundedness to the political stuff so that when the characters go off, it's against something that's plausible. And that helped a lot. It really helped. And I've gotten to know a lot of spin doctor-kinda guys, especially in *Game Change*, but in *Recount* as well. The political operatives and the political consultants are such a class of people and they have a very specific thing and every one of them is their own kind of samurai warrior self who is defined – you know each have their own – they're like superheroes. They just travel around and get hired and do different campaigns and take on different – and each of them are very different from each other and somewhat inspired by real life, too, but generally composites. As far as I know, there's no character based directly on any one character. They're all kind of inspired by a variety of people that you might recognise.'

He had assembled a formidable team – Ferrell's comedic talents were unquestioned, and Galifianakis was the semi-new kid on the block, made famous for his breakthrough role in *The Hangover*, which saw director Todd Philips take elements from *Old School* and showcase a whole new generation of talent, with Zach creating the sort of anarchic impact that Will did on *Old School*.

Roach called his lead actors 'two of the funniest, smartest guys on Earth'.

Ferrell said about his character to Collider, 'What I like about the character is what I love about the movie: we've just been able to make fun of the fertile ground that is modern-day politics. You know, I've gotten to speak in the same speech patterns as you hear where … it's just so fun – as a politician – to say [adopts politician-voice], "Thank you so much for that question. I really appreciate you. In fact, I appreciate *all* of you coming down here today. Because it's not easy. You guys have busy lives and schedules, and to carve fifteen minutes out of your day to come down here and speak face-to-face means a lot to me and the people that you report to. And you should feel good about that." [Laughter] You know, it's like …what the fuck?! I love just, like, never answering a question with a statement like that. And when we initially sat down and, you know, kind of constructed this idea, we just thought, "Boy, this would be a great opportunity to kind of comment on everything's that happening." Little did we know that we'd be in the midst of the craziest political season we probably ever had on record. So, if anything, we just hope Zach lives up to his end of the deal

[Laughter] and, you know, that he's funny. Because I know *I'll* be funny.'

He added to Collider: 'I'm focused on my hair throughout the movie, yeah. That's kind of a huge thing. And I don't know if there's anything coming, but I know there are moments where we literally reshot something because the wind was blowing and my hair was looking too crazy and it just wouldn't work for Cam. We reshot a whole *speech* so that I could have more perfect hair. That's a huge element ... which has been fun. I think someone snapped a picture of us when we were outside, and it ran in *Huffington Post* saying, "Look out, Mitt Romney, there's new hair in politics!" [Laughter] But, yeah, that was one of the first things I thought of when I thought of my character: I wanted to have this perfect, y'know, photogenic hairstyle.'

Will loved working on *The Campaign* – mainly because it got him sparring with another comedy heavyweight. It seems to spur him on when he's tackling one-liners with a formidable opponent. He told Collider: 'The times that I've gotten Zach to laugh are like high watermarks for me. And that's usually the goal, too. It'll probably never make it in the movie, but to try to make each other laugh is usually the most fun. You know, I think that's just kind of becoming the norm on comedies these days, some of the stuff that we helped kind of establish with, you know, *Anchorman* and some of the movies where you get these casts who are willing to improvise and that sort of thing. And at the same time, I mean, that becomes the headline a lot of times, which I think discounts the writing going into the process. And we also have a lot of stuff that, you know, was already written and already really funny. I mean, Jay got us here two weeks before filming and we literally sat down every day and went through every scene and kind of, you know, rehearsed them and figured out what was working or what we thought – I mean, within that process we came up with additional lines that Chris Henchy would kind of write down. So, we had this whole other playbook that we'll just open up and go to all these other alts that we came up with at rehearsal. Between what we already had and alternative stuff and stuff we come up on the spot, you know, that's why you shoot such long days.'

Will also nearly killed his co-star, telling Jon Stewart: 'We had a lot of fun. There were a lot of pranks we pulled on each other ... Zach has a nut allergy ... and so I had the craft service guy put some walnuts in his breakfast burrito and his throat closed up, to the point where they were like, "Someone call a doctor ... no seriously, someone call a doctor!" And the EMTs [Emergency Medical Technicians] came and they said, "If [we] had been five minutes later, he would have died."'

The film would make just over $100 million at the worldwide box office – a solid if unspectacular box office result. The website Badass Digest said about the film: 'Here is a film that manages to play it both broad and sharp, with lovable buffoonery by two comedy greats masking a whip-quick satire of modern politics.' However, the *New York Post* said: 'I have never seen anything as terrible as this Will Ferrell movie. Since the last Will Ferrell movie, *Casa de Mi Padre*.'

In an attempt to show off his football skills, the actor joined the Rest of the World team in the 2012 annual Soccer Aid match, which is held to raise money for Unicef. Scottish actor Gerard Butler was there, while former Manchester United star Ruud Van Nistelrooy also played. The celebs putting on the England shirt included Michael Sheen, Robbie Williams and Gordon Ramsay.

However, Will had to hobble off, recalling: 'They said, "Just run around, hit the ball and have some laughs," but everyone there had played semi-professional soccer. I popped my hamstring ... and I literally had to hobble off the field ... I had to walk the length of the field to get into the training room, and I thought the coach would be like, "I'm so sorry, I should have taken you out," but he was the former coach of Liverpool ... and his comment to me was like, "Hey Will, when I saw you hobbling off the field I was wondering if you were gonna audition for one of your Hollywood cowboy movies," and then just had a huge laugh and just walked away. I don't know if I'm ever gonna walk again at that moment.'

Will also told *Late Show* host David Letterman about his family dramas: 'The two-year-old unfortunately is just wandering into vulgarity – he has two big brothers, it wasn't from me. I'm trying to prevent it. I'm doing everything humanly possible. I'm having a good laugh and it's out of my hands, I can't control it. He thinks it's hilarious – and so do his brothers – to walk up to anyone, male or female, and say, "You have a little penis." He'll get on a roll and say it over and over again.' He added: 'My brother-in-law wants me to have a big Hollywood party and invite loads of actors, then hopefully he'll walk up to a George Clooney type and say "You have a little penis." He thinks it would be really funny.'

What would be really funny is if Will would reprise his greatest screen creation. It had been mooted for years, but lukewarm studio reaction, expected wage rises due to the star's huge subsequent success and the question of how to top the original all seemed to conspire against the demand by millions of people: 'when can we get an *Anchorman* sequel?'

Soon, would be the answer.

CHAPTER TWENTY

STILL CLASSY

In 2010, Will was asked the umpteenth time about the chances of an *Anchorman* sequel.

He said: 'It's just tough right now to get movies made. It's just weird because we were basically begged to for years and years like "Would you guys ever do a sequel? Would you ever do a sequel?" and we finally kind of were feeling it because like every year that movie has sort of built and built and built. We warmed up to the idea and we were like "That could actually be a lot of fun" and we got everyone together and then they were basically like "Great! We can't believe it! But you have to do it for this amount" and we were like "Oh, well there's no way we can do it for that." You know, it's hard to talk about budgets in Hollywood and not come off like ... because it takes a lot of money to make a movie and even a small budget is a lot of money. So I don't ever want to downplay that but if you're getting myself, Steve Carell, Paul Rudd, and probably a bunch of other people who would line up to be in that movie, it's going to cost a certain amount. But we also know we would cut everything to do it. So there really wasn't a realistic way to do it. It was basically like "Yeah! Do it for 20 dollars!" and we were like "What?" So you don't want to come off like … "Anyway, right now it's kind of like the ball is in their court, you know?" You get mad at first then you get a little frustrated then you're like "Well, if it's not meant to be then it's not meant to be and we'll go on and do something else." But, you know, I just think they come off looking strange.'

It was in 2008 that McKay and Ferrell seriously began discussing a sequel. Will has a long history of distancing himself from follow-ups, turning down a lucrative pay cheque for *Elf 2* and rubbishing follow-ups for *Old School*. But the more they talked about *Anchorman* the more excited they got. Unfortunately Paramount, who were now in control of the property after the studio's acquisitions of DreamWorks in 2005, were less keen. Then a year later they had a stroke of genius – what if they did it as a Broadway musical? Will had already enjoyed his Broadway debut, and the idea of taking it to the stage, perfecting and then filming it as a movie excited everyone.

McKay said: 'We thought we could kind of do the old Marx Brothers model where we perfected it on stage for six months, got all the jokes tight, and then we shot it. We had our story arc, we were kicking around some ideas, we even had a discussion about what we'd do at the end of the six months – would we have a replacement cast? Would people come see it if was, for instance, Alec Baldwin doing Ron Burgundy instead of Will?' However, following a discussion with Josh Gad, McKay and Ferrell became concerned. Will said: 'I was asking him about *The Book of Mormon*. I said, "I'm just curious. How long did it take for you guys to put that together?" And he was like, "Well, we workshopped it for years. We had no real idea how much work it takes to mount a musical."'

The project was eventually dropped after the budget needed for it to happen was rejected. Even when they went on to make a plan for a lower budget, it was rejected once more – no doubt not helped by *Land of the Lost*'s dismal takings. However, in 2012 they tried one more time. They were lucky, as the studio had a hole in their production schedule. McKay said: 'We were shocked. Budget wise, it was still probably 60 per cent of what we needed. Everyone had to cut their salaries quite a bit. But we were like "Screw it, let's dive in." That's kind of the spirit of the first one anyway.' It certainly wasn't the first time the screen adventures of Rob Burgundy would be faced by studio resistance. Ferrell remembered that during the first film, 'They obviously didn't get it, even when we were filming. They said, "Why would 13-year-olds care about newspeople?" We were like, "It's about broad, funny characters. It's *Austin Powers*."'

The announcement finally came on the American talk show *Conan*. Will had appeared several times on *Conan*, with one particular interview in the summer of 2012 a notable favourite, after he spawned the term 'trampire' during a joke when he appeared to be affected by the then relationship breakdown between Robert Pattinson and Kristen Stewart. 'I don't know if you follow the news at all, but there's this actress, Kristen Stewart and she goes by K-Stew, and she had a boyfriend Robert Pattinson – he's R-Patz – and she cheated on him. And they've broken up, they're not going to get back together, ever. What they had was so special, Conan, you don't even know what they had, they were in love and she just threw it all away. I don't know if there was anything I could have done to prevent this. I don't know what it means to the *Twilight* franchise. It's not going to be fine ever! [Shouting] It's never going to be fine. She is a trampire, that's what she is.'

His announcement about the sequel prompted cheers from fans when a burgundy-suited Will Ferrell, sporting shining white shoes and *that moustache*, gave the fans the good news. Ferrell appeared as Burgundy, and indulged in some banter between Conan O'Brien and his sidekick Andy Richter, before telling the audience. 'I want to announce this to everyone here in the Americas. To my friends, in Spain, Turkey and the UK, including England … as of 0900 Mountain Time, Paramount Pictures and myself, Ronald Joseph Aaron Burgundy, have come to terms on a sequel for *Anchorman*. It is official, there will be a sequel to *Anchorman*.' This after years of trying to get the project up and running after a constant tug-of-war between the cast and director and Paramount studios.

McKay let it slip to Playlist: 'Even thought it's going to be a big silly movie, it's all about the rise of the new media and 24-hour news cycles, and there's a lot of interesting points to make about that while being silly.' When asked if Ron Burgundy would get a *Mr Smith Goes To Washington*esque moment to make a rallying cry, McKay said: 'It's been discussed, there's a little wisp of [talk]. We'd never do it straight ahead, we gotta fuck with it in some way. Because Ron Burgundy isn't quite Jimmy Stewart in character, so if he does, he's not going to do it well. But there's a little bit of that going on. I mean what is this 24-hour news, and this wall of white noise information, has it really been good for our country? The great thing when you find a point of view like that is that it doesn't have to be preachy or didactic, it's also funny. It's just funny that Americans have to contend with 2000 channels, and 60 different specific news sources, and the confusion that it creates, and the junk that we get to see is hilarious. That's what we're always kinda looking for, what's the point of view that's got life to it and plays.' McKay added in another interview: 'When you read about the early days of CNN and Fox, they actually were plucking local news guys from around the country. The idea that Ron Burgundy would suddenly be on this national stage always seemed hilarious to us.'

Adam McKay tweeted in December 2012: 'It's

official. *Anchorman 2* has a release date: 20 December, 2013. Very excited.' Shortly before filming began Judd Apatow teased in an interview with *The Guardian*: 'There's no part of them [Will Ferrell and director Adam McKay] that's sweating over the pressure of making a sequel, they just wrote something that makes them laugh. It's so hilarious and unique, and satirical, I'm excited to be on it.'

Coinciding with the hype surrounding the return of Ron Burgundy, Ferrell was presented with the Comedic Genius Award at the MTV Movie Awards on 14 April 2013. He was introduced by Peter Dinklage, star of *Game of Thrones*, who joked: 'If there's one thing Will knows it's comedy. Here are some things he doesn't know. He doesn't know when to stop staring at your wife in her bikini. He doesn't know the basics of dental hygiene. He doesn't know how to flush. He doesn't know how to fart the alphabet although he will try to convince you he does. However, the one thing he does know is comedy. He's the best at it and that's why he is rightfully receiving the Comedic Genius award.' Accepting the award, Will said: 'Most of you here think I'm funny and for that I am grateful but for those of you who don't I'll fight you all in the parking lot. My friend Peter Dinklage has offered to help me fight whoever shows up to the death or until our parking meter runs out.'

However, the night nearly didn't go as planned. Aubrey Plaza, from TV show *Parks and Recreation*, appeared on stage, drink in hand, next to Ferrell and attempted to take the golden popcorn from his hands. Awkward tugging followed, before she gave it up, leaving a bemused Ferrell on stage, and awkward audience response. Her motives seemed to have been obvious when the close-up showed the title of the actress's new film, *The To-Do List*, on her chest. Ferrell told Plaza, 'Just like we rehearsed it.' However, it seems he was just playing along, as the stunt was believed to be unplanned and unrehearsed – much like the infamous Kanye West/Taylor Swift moment at the 2009 MTV Video Music Awards, when Kanye hijacked the stage to tell Taylor that Beyoncé deserved the award, not her.

Ferrell told MTV News, 'I think she wanted to tell me something important, but there was no message. It was just a lot of hot liquor breath.' MTV shows have had such stunts happen before, with Sacha Baron Cohen dropping from the ceiling and landing, crotch first, into Eminem's face, which caused the rapper to get upset. However, it later transpired to be a stunt that all players knew about. It was also pointed out that a relatively little-known actress would not have had such a prime spot at the show, and the close-up that ensured her film was promoted left people suspicious.

Befitting a film that was eagerly awaited, each casting notice about *Anchorman 2* was given great prominence on film websites and industry newspapers. The major new addition was Harrison Ford: on 4 March 2013 the *Hollywood Reporter* announced that the iconic actor would star in the sequel, as legendary newscaster Tom

Brokaw. It was a chance for Ford to sharpen his comedy chops, and he had also recently played an anchorman in the 2010 comedy-drama *Morning Glory*.

While the slow -burning success of the first *Anchorman* was impressive, there was no guarantee that the sequel would be a hit. So the film's marketing department did what every marketing department does with a seemingly bottomless budget, they marketed the hell out of it.

It seemed not a day went past during the festive season without an appearance of Will Ferrell in Burgundy guise on viral videos commenting on current news and sports events. The novelty aspect of it threatened to be short-lived due to the constant exposure, but, at the very least, this made sure that every suitable demographic target, young and old, knew of the sequel.

Despite the oversaturation of the adverts, or perhaps because of it, *Anchorman 2: The Legend Continues* didn't quite have the massive box-office opening everyone involved would have hoped. It took over $25 million in its first weekend. Not bad, but certainly not amazing, given the hype. However, just like the first movie, the box office continued to grow as the weeks went on. Within weeks it passed the $100 million mark, beating the previous film's takings and, because the film cost far less than previous Ferrell blockbusters, it will have earned a tidy profit and fully endorsed bringing back the much beloved news team. Reviews were generally positive, with Rotten Tomatoes scoring it a respectable 75 per cent. Ferrell was delighted with the reaction, and in his celebratory mood was in no rush to ease up following his next film, which was released soon afterwards.

When news first came that Will Ferrell was starring in *The Lego Movie*, it would have been fair to assume that it was going to be another soulless movie, with its only purpose seemingly to promote the hugely iconic brand. With Ferrell doing the voice of Lord Businessman – the film's villain – alongside the vocal talents of Morgan Freeman, Liam Neeson and Chris Pratt, it could have been assumed that it was a paycheck gig.

But a funny thing happened with *The Lego Movie*, and something that many never saw coming. Directed by Phil Lord and Chris Miller, the team behind the truly amazing *Cloudy With a Chance of Meatballs* and the surprise hit *21 Jump Street*, *The Lego Movie* was super-smart, wildly inventive and skewered the mass consumerism, pre-packaged, soulless mass-media culture that we live in. It instead celebrated the simple joys of playing with toys as a child. It was also incredibly funny, for both adults and kids.

But the real magic was the twist in the tale near the end – with the film becoming a live-action movie – featuring Will Ferrell as the dad who treats Lego not as a plaything, but as a constructed set of models and buildings, that must never be touched and must be built according to the strict instructions. The moving scene is brilliantly done, and manages to be memorable in a film packed with memorable scenes.

It was a blockbuster hit, scoring a $69 million

opening – the second highest February opening ever. Within the month it had earned nearly $200 million in the USA alone.

While audiences loved to see Ron Burgundy back on the big screen, Ferrell will constantly try to find new ways to engage his fans. Following *Anchorman 2*, he will also team up again with his *Anchorman* co-star Jack Black for a movie called *Tag Brothers*, according to an article in *The Wall Street Journal* written by Mark Steilen. The movie is based on a true story of a group of childhood friends who used to indulge in a game of tag while growing up. Now grown men, they started the practice up again, indulging in a game of tag one month a year, with no boundaries, and the entire world as their playground. Jumping up out of one of their car boots to tag another, conspiring with friends and families to get their man, it has become an epic game. After that month has finished, the person who is 'It' has a whole year of having the stigma of losing, before planning his comeback once the tag month is upon them.

The future is still bright for Will, and although he may take on a few risky roles, he knows where his talent lies: 'I'd rather be in a comedy. In my view, comedy wins out in the long run. I'm not sure I'm a good enough actor to play real tragedy, so I bring a comic element to most things as my answer to the world's problems. I'm not a clown though. I love goofing around, but I don't feel the need to act the clown in private – I do at work, that's where I exorcise my demons. Although I confess that I do sometimes put together outfits to annoy my wife.'

Whatever he does – whether it's on the small screen, the big screen or the Internet – he knows how to be a success. As former *SNL* member Will Forte said when introducing Will on stage for a comedy show: 'And now, the man who turned the silver screen gold – he craps box office and wipes with DVD sales – Will Ferrell.'